YORK NOTES

THE CATCHER IN THE RYE

J.D. SALINGER

NOTES BY NIGEL TOOKEY

Longman

York Press

YORK PRESS
322 Old Brompton Road, London SW5 9JH

PEARSON EDUCATION LIMITED
Edinburgh Gate, Harlow,
Essex CM20 2JE, United Kingdom
Associated companies, branches and representatives throughout the world

First published 1997
This new and fully revised edition first published 2003
15 14 13 12

ISBN: 978-0-582-77272-4

Designed by Michelle Cannatella
Illustrations by Stephen Player
Typeset by Land & Unwin (Data Sciences), Bugbrooke, Northamptonshire
Printed in China
EPC/12

CONTENTS

PREFACE

York Notes are designed to give you a broader perspective on works of literature studied at GCSE and equivalent levels. With examination requirements changing in the twenty-first century, we have made a number of significant changes to this new series. We continue to help students to reach their own interpretations of the text but York Notes now have important extra-value new features.

You will discover that York Notes are genuinely interactive. The new **Checkpoint** features make sure that you can test your knowledge and broaden your understanding. You will also be directed to excellent websites, books and films where you can follow up ideas for yourself.

The **Resources** section has been updated and an entirely new section has been devoted to how to improve your grade. Careful reading and application of the principles laid out in the Resources section guarantee improved performance.

The **Detailed summaries** include an easy-to-follow skeleton structure of the story-line, while the section on **Language and style** has been extended to offer an in-depth discussion of the writer's techniques.

The Contents page shows the structure of this study guide. However, there is no need to read from the beginning to the end as you would with a novel, play or poem. Use the Notes in the way that suits you. Our aim is to help you with your understanding of the work, not to dictate how you should learn.

Our authors are practising English teachers and examiners who have used their experience to offer a whole range of **Examiner's secrets** – useful hints to encourage exam success.

The General Editor of this series is John Polley, Senior GCSE Examiner and former Head of English at Harrow Way Community School, Andover.

The author of these Notes is Nigel Tookey, who is Head of English at a large Further Education college near London. He is an English graduate and a Senior Examiner for GCSE English.

The text used in these Notes is the 1994 Penguin Books edition.

PART ONE

INTRODUCTION

HOW TO STUDY A NOVEL

A novelist starts with a story that examines a situation and the actions of particular characters. Remember that authors are not photographers, and that a novel never resembles real life exactly. Ultimately, a novel represents a view of the world that has been created in the author's imagination.

There are six features of a novel:

❶ THE STORY: this is the series of events, deliberately organised by the writer to test the characters

❷ THE CHARACTERS: the people who have to respond to the events of the story. Since they are human, they can be good or bad, clever or stupid, likeable or detestable, etc. They may change too!

❸ THE VIEWPOINT/VOICE: who is telling the story. The viewpoint may come from one of the characters, or from an omniscient (all-seeing) narrator, which allows the novelist to write about the perspectives of all the characters

❹ THE THEMES: these are the underlying messages, or meanings, of the novel

❺ THE SETTING: this concerns the time and place that the author has chosen for the story

❻ THE LANGUAGE AND STYLE: these are the words that the author has used to influence our understanding of the novel

To arrive at the fullest understanding of a novel, you need to read it several times. In this way, you can see how all the choices the author has made add up to a particular view of life, and develop your own ideas about it.

The purpose of these York Notes is to help you understand what the novel is about and to enable you to make your own interpretation. Do not expect the study of a novel to be neat and easy: novels are chosen for examination purposes, not written for them!

EXAMINER'S SECRET
Don't say what you think the examiner wants you to say. Success follows when you give a personal response!

AUTHOR – LIFE AND WORKS

1919 1st January – Born in New York Nursery and Child's Hospital

1928 Family move to a house overlooking Central Park

1934 Enrols at Valley Forge Military Academy

1937 Visits Austria and Poland with his father to learn the family business

1939 Joins a short story-writing class run by Whit Burnett at Columbia University

1940 First story is published: 'The Young Folks' in Whit Burnett's *Story* Magazine

1942 Drafted into US army

1944 Stationed with army at Tiverton, Devon

1945 Discharged from army in November. In December first published story about *The Catcher in the Rye*

1951 *The Catcher in the Rye* is published as a novel

1953 Moves to Cornish, New Hampshire – becomes a recluse. Publishes *For Esmé – with Love and Squalor* (nine stories)

1955 Marries Claire Douglas, publishes *Raise High the Roofbeam Carpenters*, and *Seymour: an Introduction*

1961 Publishes *Franny and Zooey*

1967 Wife divorces him

1974 *Complete Uncollected Short Stories of J.D. Salinger* is published, unauthorised

At time of publication, no new novel by Salinger has been published yet

CONTEXT

1918 First World War ends in November. American troops come home

1929 The Wall Street Crash – thousands of Americans lose their savings in the stock market calamity

1934 Adolph Hitler becomes Führer of Germany. Persecution of Jews begins

1938 Germany takes over Austria

1939 Second World War begins

1941 America joins the war. Declares war on Japan, Germany and Italy

1945 Second World War ends – The leaders of America, Great Britain and the USSR meet

1950 Korean War begins, America at war again. Beginning of a period of great prosperity for America

1955 Elvis Presley releases *Heartbreak Hotel* – beginning of the Rock and Roll era.

1961 Mass CND rally in London against Nuclear weapons. Yuri Gagarin becomes first man in space

1967 The Beatles are the most popular group in the world. Homosexuality and abortion are legalised in Great Britain

1974 The Watergate Scandal breaks in America. President Nixon is forced to resign

1980 John Lennon is shot in New York by Mark Chapman, who is holding a copy of *The Catcher in the Rye*

1990 America at war in Iraq

2001 World trade Centre in New York is destroyed by terrorists

SETTING AND BACKGROUND

FAMILY BACKGROUND

- **Birth**: J.D. Salinger was born in New York City in 1919. His full name is Jerome David Salinger.

- **Parents and family**: His father, Sol Salinger, was in the food import business and his mother, Miriam Jillich, was a housewife. His writing is probably based on his own life to some extent; some of his childhood experiences seem to link to parts of *The Catcher in the Rye* although there are no really obvious connections; he had a sister who was eight years older than he, called Doris, and no brothers.

EDUCATION

- J.D. Salinger went to school in Manhattan, the same district as Phoebe's school in the novel, and his schoolwork was of average standard.

- At the age of thirteen he was sent to a school called the McBurney School where he lasted one year before 'flunking', just as Holden does in *The Catcher in the Rye.*

- At the age of fifteen his parents enrolled him in the Valley Forge Military Academy in Pennsylvania, the state where Salinger places Pencey Prep. In the novel Holden also says that his parents will probably send him to a military academy when they find out he has been expelled from Pencey Prep.

- J.D. Salinger successfully finished at Valley Forge in 1936.

LATER LIFE AND WORK

- **Early writing career**: In 1937 he joined New York University but only stayed a short while before going to Vienna with his father to learn about the family business. He came back to America after a short time and took a short story writing course. This led to his first story being published in 1940 in a magazine called *Story.*

CHECK THE BOOK

In Search of J.D. Salinger by Ian Hamilton gives a full account of J.D. Salinger's life.

- **War years:** During the Second World War J.D. Salinger worked mainly in Intelligence, but he was part of the D-day invasion force.

- **Starting on *The Catcher in The Rye*:** He came back to New York at the end of the war and lived with his parents while he was writing *The Catcher in the Rye*, which was published as a serial in a magazine between 1945 and 1946; it was first published in novel form in 1951. *The Catcher in the Rye* is his only novel, but it became a classic amongst students and young people everywhere and remains so today.

- **Life after *The Catcher in the Rye*:** He moved out of New York to various places in the countryside before settling in a town called Cornish, in the state of New Hampshire. He married a woman called Claire Douglas and they now have two children. Since the popularity of *The Catcher in the Rye* and since his marriage, J.D. Salinger has been a recluse, seeking privacy and never giving interviews to the media. He refuses to talk about his fiction and will not even allow quotations to be used from his work.

CHECK THE BOOK

Franny and Zooey deals with the relationship between a brother and sister, strongly echoing Holden and Phoebe's relationship.

- **Other books by J.D. Salinger:** All collections of his short stories were first published individually in a famous American magazine called *The New Yorker*. These include *Nine Stories*, published in 1953 and republished in the UK under the title of *For Esmé – in Love and Squalor* (this story being based on his wartime experiences in Devon). These were then followed by a series of linked stories dealing with the Glass family. Some of these are found in *Raise High the Roofbeam, Carpenters* and *Seymour: An Introduction* which is a series of stories about a bright but troubled young man, Seymour Glass, who eventually commits suicide.

PUBLISHING HISTORY

- **In America:** *The Catcher in the Rye* was first published as a serial 1945–6, and published as a book in 1951.

- **In Britain:** *The Catcher in the Rye* was originally published in London in 1951 by Hamish Hamilton, and this edition and the following edition published by Penguin were different from the original American version. Minor changes were made to the original text, for instance American spellings changed to British ones, the author's use of italic removed and words taken out like 'fuck' and 'goddam', which were unacceptable to people in the 1950s.

- In 1994 Hamish Hamilton and Penguin published the original American text, on which these Notes are based. The use of italic in this original text gives extra emphasis to Holden's phrases, for example 'They're *nice* and all' on the first page of the novel.

RESPONSE TO THE NOVEL

Initial criticism

When first published in America by Little Brown and Co. in 1951, *The Catcher in the Rye* caused instant controversy. Many reviews said it was a sensational achievement while others objected to its use of 'bad' language and the shocking nature of some of the scenes. The novel's narrator and main character, Holden Caulfield, was also thought to be a bad example to young people. In fact the novel was banned in certain areas and some education authorities condemned it.

To understand why the novel caused so much fuss, it is important to think about the time it was written and the prevailing attitudes of Americans at that time.

SOCIAL CONTEXT

American attitudes and values

The Catcher in the Rye is set just after the Second World War; America had just played a major part in helping to win the war and had become a 'superpower'. The country was very wealthy and had a huge military force; society was affluent and very materialistic. At this time, America became the first real 'consumer society'; its people were generally well off and believed that America was the greatest country in the world.

DID YOU KNOW?

The Catcher in the Rye was still banned in some places as late as 1997.

DID YOU KNOW?

In the 1950s, a 'witchhunt' against communist sympathisers was led by General McCarthy. Many leading left-wing US writers and filmmakers were unable to work.

CHECK THE FILM

Rebel without a Cause deals with a teenage rebel who is misunderstood.

However, America was also very conservative at this time and the people were often suspicious of anyone who was different from others, or who did not share their beliefs about American society's greatness; it was the beginning of the Cold War and people whose beliefs differed from the norm were often denounced as 'un-American' or 'communist sympathisers'. In *The Catcher in the Rye* Holden Caulfield rebels against some of these social attitudes and values; one small sign of this is, perhaps, Holden's red hunting hat (red being the colour associated with communism).

Rise of the teenager

The novel can also be seen as an example of the rise of teenage rebellion. Before the 1950s there was no real notion of a 'teenager'. *The Catcher in the Rye* dealt with teenagers' feelings towards the society in which they lived and became an instant success with students and young people. During the 1950s American teenagers started to make an identity for themselves and the decade saw the rise of Rock and Roll and teenage fashions. Young film actors like James Dean and Marlon Brando became huge stars with the films *Rebel Without a Cause* and *The Wild Ones*.

The start of the decade was in some ways the beginning of the 'generation gap' between teenagers and their parents and Holden Caulfield was one of its first spokespersons.

THE SETTINGS OF THE NOVEL

Pencey Prep

When the story begins we find ourselves in the enclosed little world of a boarding school with its own rules and values.

New York City

The Catcher in the Rye is an urban novel. It is set in a large city which acts as the background to Holden's story.

- Holden 'escapes' to the world of New York City, but he often finds it a frightening place; if not frightening, then full of shallow people, or 'phonies' as he calls them.

- The fact that J.D. Salinger sets his novel in a real city with recognisable landmarks and buildings adds to the sense of **realism** we feel when reading it. If we wished, we could go there and trace Holden's wanderings.

- The city represents what Holden sees as bad in the world; it is full of falsity and corruption. When Holden arrives in New York he immediately talks of the 'perverts' in the hotel where he stays. He has his encounter with the prostitute there and gets beaten up. All his worst moments occur because of the city.

- The social world of nightclubs and bars in which he spends his time are full of uncaring people with no real moral values; no one seems to have time for anybody else, everyone is thinking about themselves.

- Nearly all the city-dwellers seem flawed in some way, as if the city has corrupted them. As Holden sees it, they all let him down when he needs them:

  Sally Hayes won't run away with him.

  Carl Luce is not interested in Holden's problems.

  Even Mr Antolini is perceived by Holden as making advances to him.

  The only exception is his sister, Phoebe, who is too young to have been influenced by the values of the city.

Central Park

- The only place where Holden finds some moments of happiness is in Central Park or the museums nearby. The park is a green space, a small piece of nature in a vast, man-made environment.

- The museums represent the past, a time when things were easier and not subject to the stresses and strains of city life. In these places Holden remembers his childhood before his brother's death and his own problems; he wishes things could stay the same as they were then.

- It is in the park that he finally has a moment of true happiness, when he sees his sister riding the carrousel. It is as if these places are innocent and untainted by man. In a way the park is a

DID YOU KNOW?

J.D. Salinger's family house was near the Museum of Natural History, by Central Park.

metaphor for the wide open spaces to which Holden dreams of running away.

LITERARY TRADITIONS

Although *The Catcher in the Rye* is very much a modern, twentieth-century novel, it does have links with the literary tradition of America and of Western civilisation in general.

CHECK THE BOOK

Many people draw comparisons between *Huckleberry Finn* and *The Catcher in the Rye*.

- The narrative revolves around the idea of an individual battling with the values of the society in which he lives. This is quite a common theme throughout American literature, appearing in books like *The Scarlet Letter* by Nathaniel Hawthorne, *Huckleberry Finn* by Mark Twain and *Invisible Man* by Ralph Ellison.

- Like some of the earliest known literature, one of the central ideas in the novel is that the main character is on a quest. However, Holden's quest does not involve defeating strange monsters to get to his home, like the Ancient Greek story of Ulysses, or slaying dragons while looking for the Holy Grail, as in the stories of King Arthur. Holden's quest is to find an answer to his own problems; he is searching for his own lost innocence and for a sense of moral values.

- He is not like a traditional hero but rather an **anti-hero**, a type of character commonly found in twentieth-century fiction.

Now take a break!

PART TWO

SUMMARIES

GENERAL SUMMARY

The novel concerns three days in the life of Holden Caulfield, a troubled sixteen-year-old who has been expelled from three schools. There are frequent **flashbacks** to earlier events in Holden's life. His story is told from hospital where he is convalescing.

 DID YOU KNOW?

One of J.D. Salinger's fellow students at the Military Academy he attended said that he was full of 'wit and humour and sizzling wisecracks ... He enjoyed breaking rules'.

CHAPTERS 1–7: LEAVING PENCEY PREP

Holden's story begins on the day he leaves his school, with his farewell visit to his History teacher, Mr Spencer.

We meet Stradlater, Holden's roommate, who asks Holden to write a homework essay for him because he is taking a girl out that evening. His 'date' is Jane Gallagher, a girl Holden knows.

Holden writes the essay based on his brother Allie's baseball mitt. (Allie died of leukaemia and Holden was very disturbed by his death.) When Stradlater returns they end up fighting and this provokes Holden's early departure from school.

He decides to go to New York and stay in a hotel until returning home to his parents on the Wednesday when term officially ends and when they will have received the news of his expulsion.

CHAPTERS 8–14: THE EDMONT HOTEL

On the train he meets the mother of a fellow student. Holden lies to her about his opinion of her son.

Holden checks in to the Edmont Hotel and he goes to the hotel nightclub. He dances with three girls then goes on to another nightclub.

Back at the hotel, he makes an arrangement with the elevator-man, Maurice, for a prostitute to be sent to his room. Holden pays her but doesn't have sex. A little later the woman and Maurice return, demanding more money. Holden refuses to pay but Maurice hits Holden and they take the money by force.

CHAPTERS 15–20: FACES FROM THE PAST

Before Holden checks out of the hotel, he thinks about phoning Jane Gallagher but, instead, phones Sally Hayes. They arrange to go out that afternoon. On his way to meet her, he hears a young boy singing 'A catcher in the rye'. It cheers him.

Holden tells Sally Hayes about his problems and asks her to run away with him, but she is unsympathetic and they part company. Holden arranges to meet Carl Luce, his former student adviser. They talk but don't get on. Holden then goes to Central Park; he is very drunk and drops his sister's record, which smashes. He sits in the park feeling very depressed. Finally he leaves the park and decides to see his sister Phoebe.

CHAPTERS 21–26: REUNITED WITH PHOEBE

Holden gets into his parents' house and finds his sister. They have a long conversation during which Phoebe realises that Holden has been expelled. She becomes very upset and Holden tries to explain himself. He tells her he wants to be a 'catcher in the rye'. Eventually Holden leaves his parents' house and visits Mr Antolini's. Holden has a long conversation with him. Mr Antolini gives Holden some serious advice about his future. Holden goes to sleep and wakes up to find Mr Antolini stroking his hair. He becomes upset and rushes out of Mr Antolini's house.

Holden decides to go away and arranges to meet his sister. She arrives and explains she is going with him. He realises that this cannot happen and the turning point of the novel is reached. Holden takes his sister to the park and watches her ride on a carrousel. He now feels happy and the story ends. There is one final, brief chapter where Holden tells us he will return to school next September and that he is recovering.

DID YOU KNOW?

'Phony' means 'false' – it is one of Holden's favourite words.

DETAILED SUMMARIES

DID YOU KNOW?

We never learn why Holden is in hospital.

CHAPTER 1 – We meet Holden

1 Holden introduces himself.

2 Holden is expelled from school.

The novel opens with a young man explaining that he is going to tell us about what happened to him over one Christmas.

CHECK THE BOOK

David Copperfield is a novel by Charles Dickens. Holden obviously does not like the way in which the novel begins.

He is in a hospital near Hollywood and is talking about his brother D.B. who is a writer and has just bought a new sports car.

The first chapter sets the scene for the story and we get a sense of the character who is going to tell us the tale. We discover that the story he will tell us is only about one small part of his life, so we imagine it will be significant. In fact, the whole of the action of the novel takes place over three days, beginning on a Saturday, although Holden does spend a great deal of time recalling events from his past

The narrator says that his story began when he left his school, Pencey Prep.

It was a Saturday and an American football game was being played which was important for the school. He tells us that he was not at the game but was standing on top of Thomsen Hill looking down on the action. Holden comes across as an outsider. He begins the story on a hill away from everyone else. He tells us that the fencing team would not talk to him on the way back from New York.

> **DID YOU KNOW?**
> American public schools are what we call 'state schools'.

Holden the outsider

It is significant that the first time we meet Holden he is on his own. He has also fallen out with a team. There are many points in the novel where Holden is on his own and where he has fights or arguments with people who are trying to help him.

He was on his way to say goodbye to his History teacher. He had been expelled from school and that is the reason he had to leave. He remembers an earlier episode when he was playing football with two schoolfriends and was told to go inside by the Biology teacher, Mr Zambesi; this sort of memory helps him to say goodbye to the school. We find out about Holden's attitudes to his school and learn something about his feelings. He hates the movies and other things like advertising and publicity.

He runs towards his History teacher's house, remembering how he stopped to catch his breath and the fierce cold. Mrs Spencer, the History teacher's wife, answers the door and it is only at this point that we discover the narrator's name is Holden. He goes into the house and asks how Mr Spencer is. Holden goes to say goodbye to his History teacher and this is one of the first places in the novel where we find Holden looking for companionship. He seems drawn to adults throughout the novel, as if they will help him understand his problems, but none of the encounters really works out.

> **CHECKPOINT 1**
> Think about why the writer waits until the end of the chapter to reveal Holden's name.

The most important piece of information we learn is that Holden has been kicked out of school. He has not done anything particularly bad but just seems unable to work hard enough.

CHAPTER 2 – Holden's school history

① **We find out about Mr Spencer.**

② **Holden's parents don't know he's been expelled.**

③ **More on Holden's background is revealed.**

Holden tells us that Mr and Mrs Spencer are seventy years old. He goes on to describe Mr Spencer in the classroom and seems to feel sorry for him being so old. He talks about Mr Spencer getting enjoyment out of buying an old blanket from some American Indians. We find out some of Holden's own history while he is talking to his History teacher. Holden seems to have had a troubled time at school without doing anything really bad; it seems as if he just cannot be bothered. He is an unsettled and restless person and this theme of restlessness continues throughout the novel.

CHECK THE FILM
Dead Poets Society gives an idea of what American private schools were like.

At this point we find out that Holden's surname is Caulfield as this is what Mr Spencer calls him. Holden feels sorry he has come to Mr Spencer's house and describes the medicines surrounding Mr Spencer, saying the scene makes him depressed. Mr Spencer asks Holden why he isn't at the football game and Holden explains why.

At this point Mr Spencer starts to question Holden about recent events and asks if Holden's parents know he has been expelled yet. Holden says no and then explains to Mr Spencer that Pencey Prep is the fourth school he has attended. Holden reveals to us that he is seventeen years old but sometimes acts much younger.

Mr Spencer starts to quiz Holden about his attitude to school. Spencer tells Holden why he had to fail him in History and we learn that Holden has not really studied for any of his subjects. Spencer reads Holden's History exam answers to him which makes Holden feel uncomfortable.

> **CHECKPOINT 2**
> Give some reasons why Holden does not try at school.

We realise that Holden is worried about his parents' reaction to being expelled and get the first real idea that Holden is unhappy; he mentions being depressed three times in the chapter. Mr Spencer seems to want to help Holden but cannot understand him and this is how many of the people that Holden meets in the novel react to him.

> **CHECKPOINT 3**
> Why do people have trouble understanding Holden?

Holden talks to Mr Spencer but at the same time is daydreaming about where the ducks in Central Park go when the lake freezes over. Keep in mind Holden's remarks about where the ducks in Central Park (see map on p. 13) go in winter; this question is repeated by Holden to various people he encounters.

We discover that Holden's home is in New York. We find out the names of two of Holden's previous schools: Whooton and Elkton Hills. Holden tells us he left Elkton Hills because it was full of 'phonies'. Mr Spencer asks Holden if he is worried about his future and Holden starts to feel depressed, decides he has to go and makes an excuse to leave, lying to Mr Spencer and telling him he has to go to the gym.

 DID YOU KNOW?
'Shoot the bull' is American slang for 'pretending to be sincere'.

CHAPTER 3 – Holden and his schoolmates

❶ Holden tells us of some books he's read.

❷ We meet Ackley and Stradlater.

Holden tells us he lies a lot of the time. He describes where he lived at Pencey and relates a story about Ossenburger, a man who donated a lot of money to the school. He is quite sarcastic about him and also tells us about when one of his schoolfriends farted during Ossenburger's speech. In this chapter we understand more about the sort of people whom Holden thinks are phony. He dislikes Ossenburger because he tries to buy social status, and is quite scathing about his business. Again Holden reveals his schoolboyish, immature side when he tells the story about Edgar Marsalla.

DID YOU KNOW?

The colour of Holden's hat is **symbolic** of communism, an anti-American political system.

After leaving the Spencers' house, Holden goes back to his room which he shares with Ward Stradlater. He puts on a hat and settles down to read. When Holden tells us about his hat it does not seem to be a very important piece of information. However, this is one of the ways the writer gets us to think about Holden as someone 'different'. (You might notice that Holden wears his hat much like youths today wear their baseball caps!) The hat is frequently mentioned throughout the novel.

Holden gives us his opinion on some of the books he has read. He is interrupted by Robert Ackley, a boy who has the room next door to his. Holden describes Ackley in an unflattering way and says he is 'peculiar'. Ackley starts talking to Holden and picks up a picture of a girl called Sally Hayes whom Holden used to see in New York.

Holden tells Ackley about the fencing trip and Holden eventually has to give up trying to read his book as Ackley hangs around in his room. Holden starts play-acting as he knows this will annoy Ackley. Then Holden tells Ackley about where he bought his hat. He lends Ackley some scissors and complains when Ackley cuts his nails over the floor.

They go on to talk about Stradlater and which girl he is taking out that night. Ackley explains why he hates Stradlater. Holden changes the subject and complains once again about Ackley cutting his nails over the floor.

Stradlater comes in and asks to borrow one of Holden's jackets. At this point Ackley leaves the room. Stradlater goes to shave and Holden is left on his own.

We learn quite a lot about how Holden relates to people his own age by his descriptions of Ackley and Stradlater and their conversations. Holden likes to play the fool and we see more extreme examples of his tendency to fantasise later in the novel.

> **DID YOU KNOW?**
>
> Someone else at the Military Academy thought Salinger was 'pasty-faced, not too well-liked … a sort of "wise-guy"'.

CHAPTER 4 – Holden and Jane Gallagher

1 Holden talks to Stradlater.

2 We learn that Holden is talented at English.

3 Holden tells us about Jane Gallagher.

Holden goes to the bathroom to talk to Stradlater while he is shaving. Stradlater asks Holden to do him a favour and write his English homework for him which Holden thinks is **ironic** as he is the one being thrown out of school. Holden starts play-acting in front of Stradlater, imitating a character from a film. During Holden's meeting with Stradlater we find out that Holden is gifted at English; this idea is reinforced several times in the novel when Holden talks about the books he reads and expresses his opinions of them.

We find more evidence in this chapter of Holden's tendency to act out fantasies.

Stradlater asks Holden where he got his hat and then asks again if Holden will do his English homework for him. Holden says he will if he has time.

> ## Holden's fantasies
>
> At many points in the book, Holden fantasises about being someone from the movies or talks about characters in books he's read. This shows us that Holden is an imaginative boy and also links him with his brother D.B., who is a writer. It also demonstates that Holden contradicts himself often. He has told us he hates the movies but then fantasises about being in them. One of the key features of Holden's character is his yearning for a better life than the one he has.

He quizzes Stradlater about his date for the night, asking him which girl he is taking out. When Stradlater tells him it is Jane Gallagher, Holden gets very excited as she is a girl with whom he spent some time two summers before. Holden gets more excited and tells Stradlater he feels he should go and meet her. He reveals that he used to play draughts with her all summer. Stradlater shows no interest in Holden's memories of the girl.

Holden continues to tell Stradlater he should go and say hello to Jane Gallagher but eventually decides he is not in the mood. Stradlater is still getting ready to go out while Holden keeps questioning him about where he is taking Jane. He asks Stradlater not to tell Jane that he has been expelled. Holden starts to get nervous. He seems worried about what Stradlater and Jane will get up to. We find out that Holden thinks Stradlater is rather obsessed with sex.

DID YOU KNOW?

'Can' is slang for 'toilet'.

There is a sense of Holden yearning for a time in his past which he feels was better than now. He is nostalgic about his time with Jane Gallagher and in a way seems quite protective about her: he explains about her childhood being unhappy and worries excessively over whether Stradlater will behave when on his date with her.

CHECKPOINT 4

Note how the author creates a link between Jane and Holden's childhood.

Ackley comes back into the room and Holden is pleased to see him as he believes it will stop him thinking about Stradlater and Jane Gallagher. Ackley stays until dinnertime.

CHAPTER 5 – A tragedy in Holden's family

❶ **We learn about life at the boarding school.**

❷ **Holden tells us about his dead younger brother.**

Holden tells us about the meal at Pencey on Saturday nights and explains why the food is always steak. He goes outside after dinner with some other boys and they start playing snowballs. After this, Holden decides to go into town with his friend Mal Brossard for a hamburger and, possibly, to see a film. Once again we find Holden contradicting himself, continuing to say he hates the movies but being prepared to go there. Most of the time he complains about Ackley and deliberately tries to annoy him, yet he asks if Ackley wants to go to the movies. This is one way the writer conveys the sense that Holden is a rather mixed-up young man, unsure of what he really thinks.

Holden asks if Mal minds Ackley joining them. They go into town but do not go to the cinema. Holden cannot be bothered to see the film and they return to Pencey early.

Ackley hangs around in Holden's room and tells a story about a girl he went out with. Holden does not believe Ackley's claims about

EXAMINER'S SECRET
Jot down in a notebook all the patterns of a character's behaviour. This will give you a clearer understanding of them.

what he and the girl got up to and wants him to go. Eventually Holden tells Ackley that he has to write Stradlater's English essay and Ackley leaves.

Holden decides to write a descriptive essay about his brother Allie's baseball glove which had poems written on it. We discover that Holden's brother died of leukaemia on 18 July 1946. Holden talks fondly of him and says how intelligent and well liked he was by everyone. We find out how badly affected Holden was by his brother's death; his parents were going to send him to a psychiatrist after he broke all the windows in the family's garage. Holden tells us that his hand was damaged and has never fully healed.

DID YOU KNOW?

At college, Salinger was a loner, who had no friends, though the girls were impressed by his dark good looks. He quit after a few months.

Holden's younger brother

The introduction into the story of the subject of Holden's dead brother is crucial. Holden's description of his brother makes Allie sound almost perfect and Holden's actions after his death seem out of his own control; he is enraged that his brother has died when he seemed such a good person.

We can imagine that Allie's death was perhaps the point when Holden started to do badly at school. In several instances later in the novel when Holden is frightened or depressed he holds imaginary conversations with his dead brother, for example, at the beginning of Chapter 14 after his experience with the prostitute and in Chapter 25 when he thinks he is going to disappear.

This device is used by J.D. Salinger to keep reminding us of the importance of Allie's death to Holden and it creates a strong sense of this event's continuing effect on Holden's state of mind.

Holden writes the essay and then stares out of the window telling us he could hear Ackley snoring. He describes all of Ackley's ailments and says he feels sorry for him. In this chapter we realise that Holden is not so cynical as he has appeared so far. He does have a caring side, revealed when he tells us about his brother and when he feels sorry for Ackley.

CHAPTER 6 – A quarrel

1 Holden's essay is not to Stradlater's liking.

2 Holden is unnerved when he finds out Stradlater is dating a girl he knew.

3 They fight.

Holden, as narrator, is trying to remember what happened when Stradlater returned from his date with Jane Gallagher. There are some details that Holden cannot remember, such as where he was sitting when Stradlater came in.

Stradlater returns and asks Holden if he has written his English essay for him. When he has read it he complains to Holden that it is not the type of essay he asked for and gets very angry with Holden. Holden takes the essay from Stradlater, tears it up and throws the pieces into a rubbish bin.

Holden lights a cigarette to annoy Stradlater who then complains. Holden ignores him. They start talking about Stradlater's date with Jane. Holden tells us how much he hated Stradlater at this point. There are two things in this chapter which make Holden lose his temper with Stradlater. One is the complaint about the English essay and the second is his concern about Jane Gallagher.

Holden tears up the essay in anger because Stradlater has shown no gratitude for his efforts but also, perhaps, because it has brought back painful memories about his brother Allie.

Holden becomes very worried about what has happened between Stradlater and Jane and accuses Stradlater of having sex with her in the car which he borrowed from Ed Banky, the school basketball coach. Eventually he loses control of his emotions and swings at Stradlater, even though he has already mentioned that Stradlater is older and stronger than he is Holden remembers vaguely that he tried to hit Stradlater but missed. Stradlater pins Holden down and tries to calm him, but Holden starts insulting Stradlater. When

CHECKPOINT 5

Think of another instance where Holden gets into a fight. Note that he always comes off worst!

DID YOU KNOW?

The word 'socks' is slang for 'punches'.

CHECKPOINT 6

Do you think Holden's attack on Stradlater was caused by jealousy?

Holden refuses to keep quiet, Stradlater hits him and gives him a nose bleed.

Stradlater leaves the room because Holden keeps calling him names. Holden puts on his red hat and looks at his face in the mirror. He explains he has only been in two fights before and 'lost' them both. He goes into Ackley's room.

Holden seems concerned about Jane losing the innocence she had when he knew her and thinks that Stradlater will corrupt her in some way. He comes across like the concerned father of a teenage daughter. We are reminded here of when, in Chapter 2, Holden tells us at times he acts younger than his age and sometimes older.

CHAPTER 7 – Holden leaves Pencey Prep

❶ **Holden goes to see Ackley but is unable to confide in him.**

❷ **Holden leaves the school.**

When Ackley sees all the blood on Holden's face, he asks him what has happened. Holden explains briefly and asks Ackley if he wants to play cards. Ackley persists in asking Holden for more details about the fight but Holden refuses to tell him. Instead he lies and tells Ackley that he was fighting Stradlater on his behalf, but quickly admits he is kidding.

During this chapter Holden reveals a lot about the way he feels. He does not seem to have any real friends. Even though he goes to Ackley's room after the fight, he is sarcastic towards him and tells us he is stupid. Perhaps Holden wants some sympathy and kindness but Ackley is not sensitive to this.

Holden lies down on Ackley's roommate's bed and tells us he feels lonely. He starts to imagine Jane and Stradlater in the car and becomes very depressed. Ackley falls asleep but Holden lies awake.

He tells us a story about when he went out with Stradlater and two girls and how Stradlater tried to seduce one of them.

Feeling lonely again, Holden wakes Ackley up to talk about how to join a monastery. When Ackley gets annoyed Holden says goodbye to him sarcastically. He decides to leave Pencey right then and rent an hotel room in New York, instead of waiting until the end of term three days later. He thinks about what his mother will say when she gets the headmaster's letter saying he has been expelled.

Holden packs his bags and feels guilty when he packs the new ice-skates his mother sent him. He counts his money and decides to wake up a schoolfriend to get more money by selling his typewriter. He leaves the school, shouting an insult to the sleeping students.

The idea of Holden as a 'loner' is given added weight by the writer. The last person Holden sees at Pencey is Ackley, someone who has no friends at school and who is different from the others. While Holden shows a dislike of Ackley he also feels sorry for him. It is as if Holden realises that no one cares about Ackley, just as he feels no one cares about himself.

Holden's departure

This chapter marks the end of the initial part of the book. Holden's decision to run away to New York is prompted by his inability to cope with his own feelings, particularly about Stradlater and Jane. It is as if Holden's memory of happy times with Jane has been spoilt by Stradlater and he cannot get the image of Stradlater with Jane out of his mind.

Like many teenagers Holden has difficulty in seeing the consequences of his actions. This tendency is shown in other parts of the book; for example the encounter with the young prostitute in Chapter 13 and his ideas about running away with Sally Hayes in Chapter 17.

Now take a break!

CHECKPOINT 7
Holden talks about sex in very vague terms. Give reasons for this.

 DID YOU KNOW?
'It killed me' here means annoyed me. At most other times Holden uses it to mean 'amused me'.

TEST YOURSELF (CHAPTERS 1–7)

WHO ARE?

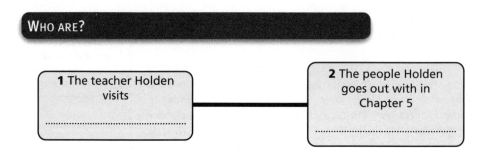

1 The teacher Holden visits

....

2 The people Holden goes out with in Chapter 5

....

LOCATE THE FOLLOWING

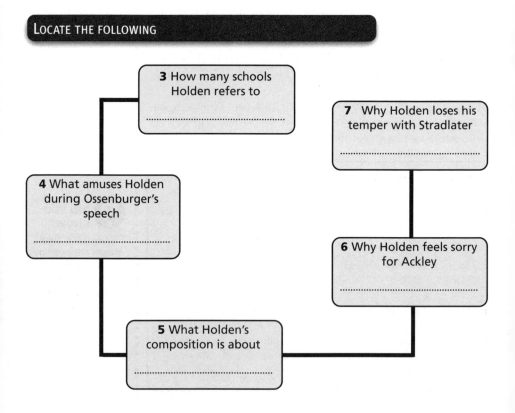

3 How many schools Holden refers to

....

7 Why Holden loses his temper with Stradlater

....

4 What amuses Holden during Ossenburger's speech

....

6 Why Holden feels sorry for Ackley

....

5 What Holden's composition is about

....

Check your answers on p. 98.

CHAPTER 8 – The train to New York

1 Holden meets Ernest Morrow's mother.

2 We hear more about Holden's tendency to lie.

On leaving Pencey, Holden walks to the station and catches a train to New York. He tells us that he usually enjoys train journeys. After Holden has been on the train for a short time a woman gets on. She is the mother of Ernest Morrow, one of the students Holden knew at Pencey.

The woman notices a Pencey Prep sticker on Holden's luggage and strikes up a conversation with him about the school. Holden tells us that her son was one of the students he most disliked but he pretends to the woman that he liked him. Holden lies about his name to Mrs Morrow and tells her it is Rudolph Schmidt, the name of the school caretaker. Holden notices the woman's jewellery and goes on to say she is attractive. We find more evidence in this chapter of Holden's tendency to lie.

CHECKPOINT 8

Think about the reasons for Holden's tendency to lie.

This seems closely linked with the way he play-acts. His lies to Mrs Morrow are to protect himself but also to make her feel good about her son. He also tells us he feels guilty about lying.

The conversation with Mrs Morrow carries on and Holden tells her that he and some of the other boys wanted to elect Ernest class president. Holden is complimentary to Mrs Morrow, even though he is informing us how much he dislikes her son. We could think Holden insincere, something he accuses other people of being when he calls them 'phonies'.

Holden invites Mrs Morrow for a drink. He tells her he can get served because he has some grey hair, making him look older than he is. She tells him the bar will be closed. This is the first meeting with an adult after Holden has left Pencey. Notice how Holden tries to act like an adult, or at least how he thinks an adult would act. He offers her cigarettes and invites her for a drink.

Mrs Morrow asks Holden why he is going home before the end of term and Holden lies again, telling her he has to have an operation on a small brain tumour. Mrs Morrow is horrified but Holden says it isn't serious. They say goodbye and she invites him to spend some of the summer with her and Ernest; Holden tells us this is the last thing he would want to do.

CHAPTER 9 – Holden arrives in New York

❶ Holden takes a taxi to the Edmont Hotel.

❷ Scenes from hotel bedrooms are described.

❸ Holden phones a 'stripper'.

When Holden arrives in New York the first thing he wants to do is phone someone but he cannot decide who to phone. He takes a taxi but absent-mindedly gives his home address; he tells the taxi driver he has made a mistake. Holden asks the driver about the ducks on the lake in Central Park but the driver just thinks he is strange. The writer creates an **image** of escape with this reference to the ducks, which could represent Holden's own 'flight' from school. Holden tells the driver to take him to the Edmont Hotel, taking off his red hat before checking in.

Holden is given a room overlooking the other side of the hotel, but he says he is too depressed to care. He describes a man dressing up in women's clothes, whom he can see in one of the rooms opposite. He also sees a man and a woman squirting water at each other from their mouths. Holden calls them 'perverts' and says he is the only normal person there. He thinks of Stradlater, saying he would love the hotel.

Holden, women and sex

Holden's views on women and sex form quite a large part of this chapter. He seems confused and, in one way, disgusted by sexual activity. The people he sees from his room disgust him and his own attempts to persuade the girl on the phone out for cocktails fail. This is all evidence of Holden's struggle to deal with the period between childhood and adulthood.

Holden's relations with women are also raised by his thought about phoning Jane Gallagher, his night with the three girls in the Lavender Club and his unsatisfactory date with Sally Hayes. Holden seems unable to connect with the opposite sex and this emphasises his loneliness. This theme of his inability to connect with anyone (see **Themes** on **Relationships**) runs through most of the novel.

Holden thinks about his feelings regarding sex and admits he doesn't understand it. He considers ringing Jane Gallagher but says he isn't in the mood. Holden feels like meeting a woman and remembers a phone number of a woman he thinks used to be a stripper, given to him by an acquaintance.

Although it is very late Holden phones the woman, who is angry at being woken. When she finds out that Holden's acquaintance went to an expensive private college she becomes more friendly but still will not come out that night. She asks Holden if she can meet him the next night but he refuses. Immediately he regrets it but they hang up. He thinks he has handled the situation badly. The idea that Holden seems desperate for company is reinforced by his:

CHECKPOINT 9

Note how often Holden thinks about phoning Jane Gallagher. Think about why he never ends up speaking to her.

- Wanting to phone someone from the station
- Asking the taxi driver if he would like a cocktail with him, even though he has never seen him before
- Phoning the girl so late at night.

CHAPTER 10 – Holden in the Lavender Room

1 Phoebe is described by Holden.

2 Holden meets three girls in the nightclub.

3 The girls tease Holden.

Holden decides to go down to the hotel nightclub, the Lavender Room. While changing he thinks about phoning Phoebe, his little sister, but is too frightened of his parents answering.

CHECKPOINT 10

What links Holden, Phoebe and D.B.?

Holden, speaking affectionately about his sister, tells us that she is pretty and understanding. He mentions her favourite film, *The 39 Steps*, and tells us she knows the dialogue by heart. He says she likes to write stories. Holden remembers when he and his brother Allie used to take her to the park and how much Allie liked her. The memories of Phoebe, which occupy Holden's thoughts at the beginning of the chapter, make us think of her as a **symbol** for him of what was good about family life. However, he is still too afraid of his parents' reactions to risk phoning home. Holden's urge to see Phoebe becomes stronger as the story progresses.

Holden enters the Lavender Room and tries to buy an alcoholic drink but is refused. When Holden orders a drink and is refused service, we realise how easy it is for people to see he is just a young man and not the 'adult' he tries to be. He starts talking to three girls, offering to dance with them one at a time. One of them dances with him and he tells us what a good dancer she was. While Holden is dancing with her he tries to talk to her but she is not interested. They sit down and Holden gives his name as Jim Steele.

Holden tells us he danced with all three of the girls and that one of them was a bad dancer. To amuse himself, he pretends to have seen a movie star in the club. The girl returns to her friends and repeats what Holden has just told her, which amuses him.

Holden buys the girls two drinks each before the bar closes. One of the girls teases Holden about his age and shortly after this they leave. He pays the bill and is annoyed that the girls did not offer anything towards the drinks but then says he wouldn't have accepted their money anyway. He leaves the Lavender Room.

We find more evidence of the contradictions between what Holden reveals to us and what he says to the people he meets. He is polite to the girls he meets and seems to want to spend time with them, but he constantly tells us what 'morons' they were. The encounter could also be seen as more evidence of Holden's loneliness.

DID YOU KNOW?

In Greek mythology Phoebe (also called Artemis) was Apollo's twin sister, associated with light and wisdom.

DID YOU KNOW?

'Grools' is American slang for 'stupid, ugly people'.

CHAPTER 11 – Holden's memories of Jane Gallagher

① Holden reminisces about Jane.

② He takes a taxi to another nightclub.

CHECKPOINT 11

Why do you think it is significant that Holden has shown Jane his brother's baseball mitt?

As Holden goes into the hotel lobby he starts to think of Jane Gallagher again. The thought of her and Stradlater in the car still upsets him. He talks about when he got to know Jane and how they spent a summer together. Holden describes Jane's appearance and reveals that she is the only other person to whom he has shown Allie's baseball mitt. Nearly the whole of the chapter is taken up with Holden's memories of Jane. Once again, we see Holden being nostalgic about the past when life seemed better for him.

Holden tells us about a specific incident when he and Jane came close to kissing. The story involves Jane getting upset about her stepfather, Mr Cudahy. Holden describes him as a 'booze-hound' and says how Jane refused to speak to him and how when he left she started crying. Holden tried to comfort her and in the process started kissing her face but, he stresses, not on her mouth.

Holden and Jane

Although we never actually meet Jane Gallagher in the novel she is repeatedly mentioned. Holden thinks about phoning her throughout the book and even does so on a couple of occasions. However, he never gets to speak to her.

Holden explains that Jane was a warm and affectionate person and different from other girls. He talks about going to the movies with her. As he is thinking about this, the memory of her and Stradlater returns again. Even though Holden is sure Jane would not have done anything physical with Stradlater, the thought still upsets him.

The writer reveals to us Holden's caring side, showing him to be a complex character. Holden is still genuinely concerned about Jane and remembers fondly their time together.

He seems to have a lot in common with her; for example, they both have unhappiness in their childhood, she is 'different' just like Holden and they enjoy doing the same things together. Jane seems to represent Holden's perfect girl.

Holden is not tired and decides to get a taxi to a nightclub called Ernie's where his brother D.B. used to go before moving to Hollywood. He tells us about the piano player at the club.

CHAPTER 12 – Holden about town

① **Holden takes another taxi ride.**

② **Ernie and the nightclub are described.**

③ **We learn more about Holden being depressed.**

Holden gets in the taxi and says how depressing the city looks from the streets. He wishes he could go home and see his sister Phoebe. He starts talking to the driver about the ducks on the lake. The driver says he does not know the answer but begins a strange conversation about what happens to the fish in the lake during winter. Holden invites the driver for a drink even though he has told us he is the 'touchiest guy' he has ever come across. The driver refuses.

Note that Chapter 11 ends by Holden deciding to take a taxi and describing Ernie at the club, and then Chapter 12 begins by jumping back to the taxi-ride on the way to the club. This use of **flashback** is typical of a conversational, **episodic** story (see **Structure**).

The events in the taxi are almost identical to the previous ride Holden took. What is different is that this driver engages him in conversation. Holden argues about the fish in the lake but gives up because the driver seems to be angry. In a way, the conversation indicates how Holden tries to communicate with people but often fails. He is misunderstood in more ways than one.

On entering the club, Holden tells us it is packed with college students. He talks about Ernie, the piano player, whom he has already described in Chapter 11, saying he was messing up the song being played but that the audience still loved it. He thinks the

DID YOU KNOW?
'Ice-cold hot licks' is slang for 'poor trumpet solos'.

situation is 'phony' and it depresses him; however, he does not leave because he does not want to be alone.

CHECKPOINT 12

Identify what Holden thinks is phony about the club.

Holden is shown to a bad table but is served with alcohol. He explains that no one there cares about underage drinking. After seeing the caring side of Holden in the last chapter we witness more of his sarcastic side in the nightclub. He is scathing about all aspects of the club, complaining that everything about the place is phony. He claims it depresses him, just as the streets of New York have done earlier. Holden sits and listens to people's conversations, telling us they are all 'jerks'. He dislikes everything he hears.

Suddenly, one of his brother's old girlfriends, Lillian Simmons, appears and starts talking to Holden about his brother. She introduces her boyfriend and invites Holden to join them for a drink. Holden refuses and lies to her, saying he has to meet someone. He leaves the club.

Holden complains about being on his own in the club but when someone invites him to join them he refuses; he seems awkward and does not want to talk about his brother.

 DID YOU KNOW?

'Tossed his cookies' is American slang for 'being sick'.

In this chapter our impression of Holden as an outsider is made stronger by the writer contrasting his dislike of the club with the fact that everyone else there is enjoying themselves.

CHAPTER 13 – Holden and the prostitute

1 Holden becomes more depressed.

2 Holden has an encounter with a prostitute.

Holden walks back quite a distance to the hotel. He tells us again how cold it was and starts daydreaming about what he would have said to whoever stole his gloves at Pencey. He pretends briefly that he would have acted tough but admits he is a bit of a coward and would probably have done nothing.

These thoughts make him depressed and he decides to stop off for another drink. He brags about how much he can drink, saying it doesn't affect him, but decides against going into the bar.

When he gets back to the hotel, he feels very depressed. He gets in the elevator where the person operating it asks him if he wants a woman for the night. Holden lies about his age, saying he's twenty-two, and accepts the offer. He tells us it is against his principles but that he was too depressed to think straight. The man says he will send the girl up to Holden's room in fifteen minutes, after having told him it will cost five dollars.

DID YOU KNOW?
'A little tail' is slang for 'sex with a woman', and 'a throw' is 'an act of sexual intercourse'.

Holden's depression

Holden talks about his depression more and more as this section of the novel progresses. It is these feelings of sadness and loneliness which lead to him agreeing to see the prostitute.

Note carefully how Salinger develops Holden's feelings. Holden seems to think that if he does things which are supposed to be enjoyable and which he associates with being an adult male then his depression will go away. This also explains his outings to nightclubs and his drinking.

The scene with the prostitute is especially significant because it shows us that Holden is still a boy. It marks the end of his attempts to appear 'grown up'.

The scene with the prostitute also gives us an important insight into Holden's moral attitudes. He accepts the elevator-man's offer of a prostitute because he wants to appear as a carefree 'man about town', enjoying life and with money to spend. Almost as soon as he has done this he regrets it and we find out about his innocence with regard to sex.

CHECK THE BOOK

The writers Salinger used to be most frequently compared to were Scott Fitzgerald and Ring Lardner.

Holden waits in his room and changes his clothes. He admits that he is a virgin and tells us he is nervous. He thinks about a book he once read about someone who was a womaniser but says he wouldn't be like that.

The prostitute arrives and Holden quickly realises she is about the same age as he is. Holden tells her he is twenty-two but she does not believe him. As they talk the girl pulls her dress off, which shocks Holden. He feels embarrassed and 'peculiar' and tries to make conversation with the girl. His attempts to have a conversation with the girl fail, reinforcing the idea that Holden wants to communicate meaningfully with someone but cannot. With one or two exceptions, nobody he meets seems interested in him as a person.

The prostitute is not interested in talking and Holden finally admits he doesn't feel like sex. Holden sees how young she is, he feels sorry for her. Holden sees her world as sad and corrupt. He realises he cannot have sex with her and vaguely describes his feelings. It is as if he does not know the words to describe his emotions at that moment and this shows his innocence again.

He makes up a story that he has recently had an operation and then pays the prostitute. She says to him he should give her ten dollars but Holden says the elevator-man said five. She leaves the room.

Holden's tendencies to act out fantasies are shown again in this chapter. He pretends to be a 'tough guy' at the beginning of the chapter and tries, but fails, to act like a 'macho' man in the scene with the prostitute.

CHAPTER 14 – Holden is beaten up

❶ Holden talks to Allie.

❷ Maurice and Sunny get more money from Holden.

❸ We read more of Holden's fantasies.

Holden sits in his room; it is dawn on Sunday morning. He feels very depressed and starts an imaginary conversation with his brother Allie. Holden's imaginary conversation with Allie represents an attempt to counter his depression. He imagines putting right a time when he let his brother down.

After Holden has got into bed he starts telling us his views on the Bible; he reveals that he likes Jesus but not the disciples and tells us he is an atheist. The subject of Jesus, which occurs so soon after Holden's encounter with the prostitute, could be seen as a way of introducing Holden's guilt at what he has done. He knows his actions are 'sinful' according to the Bible and, even though he claims to be an atheist, the introduction of religion into his thoughts is significant.

There is a knock on Holden's door. It is Maurice, the elevator-man, and the prostitute, Sunny, who demand more money from Holden. He refuses to pay and Maurice threatens him. Holden says he will call the police but Maurice dissuades him, asking him if he would want his parents to know he had been with a prostitute. While Holden struggles with Maurice, Sunny finds Holden's wallet and takes out the extra five dollars they are demanding. Holden starts crying and calls Maurice a 'moron'. Maurice and the girl leave after he has punched Holden in the stomach.

The idea that Holden is a boy in a man's world is reinforced by the fight scene with Maurice. Holden cannot stop Maurice and Sunny taking the money and his reactions are those of a child: he cries and hurls insults, just as he did with Stradlater.

Holden lies on the floor as he did when Stradlater hit him. He then

DID YOU KNOW?

At the time J.D. Salinger wrote this novel, western society was much more religious than it is today, and would have found Holden's 'atheism' shocking.

Chapter 14 continued

walks to the bathroom, telling us he was in a lot of pain. He goes into another of his fantasies, pretending to have been shot in the stomach and then getting his revenge by shooting Maurice. He blames his fantasising on the movies.

 DID YOU KNOW?

Teenagers are the age group most likely to commit suicide.

At the end of the chapter Holden tells us he is so depressed he feels like killing himself. Holden's comments reveal how desperate he has become. The events that have taken place over the Saturday night reveal Holden to be a very young man who cannot cope with the adult world he is trying to inhabit and who is saddened by the people he meets.

Now take a break!

WHO ARE?

1 The woman Holden meets on the train to New York

....

4 The prostitute Holden sees

....

2 The girls with whom Holden dances

....

3 The piano player at the club

....

LOCATE THE FOLLOWING

5 The names of the nightclubs Holden visits

....

6 Where Holden and Jane spent time together

....

7 The reason for Holden's fight with the elevator-man

....

Check your answers on p. 98.

CHAPTER 15 – Holden makes a date

❶ Holden makes a date with Sally Hayes and checks out of the Egmont Hotel.

❷ We learn something about his parents.

❸ Holden meets some nuns.

At ten o'clock Holden wakes up and feels hungry but does not send out for any food as he is frightened that Maurice may bring it. He thinks about phoning Jane but again decides that he is not in the mood. We sense that he is frightened that by talking to her now it will spoil his memories of her. He could also be worried about what she may say about her and Stradlater.

Holden phones Sally Hayes and arranges to meet her at two o'clock. When Holden makes a date with Sally Hayes it seems as though she is a substitute for the person Holden really wants to see.

He checks out of the hotel and takes a taxi to Grand Central Station to leave his bags in the left luggage facility. On the way there he gives us a little information about his father and mother, telling us that his father is a wealthy lawyer and that his mother has not been well since Allie's death.

CHECK THE BOOK

Romeo and Juliet also tells the story of young people rebelling against their society.

CHECKPOINT 13

Think of some reasons why Holden admires the nuns.

While having breakfast at the railway station, Holden meets two nuns and gives them ten dollars towards charity. We see Holden's generosity in his donation to the nuns. Money seems unimportant to him – perhaps because of his wealthy father? He starts a conversation with them. He discovers that one is an English teacher and they talk for quite a while about books Holden has read. They discuss *Romeo and Juliet*. Holden reveals more to us about his knowledge of English literature when he talks about *Romeo and Juliet*. It makes us wonder again why an intelligent young person should keep getting thrown out of school, the reason for his current plight.

When the nuns have gone, Holden tells us he enjoyed talking to them. The conversation with the nuns is one of the few in the novel where Holden is himself and not putting on an act or lying. This could be the reason why he enjoys talking to them. Holden wishes he had given the nuns a bigger donation and tells us that money makes you miserable.

DID YOU KNOW?

Grand Central Station is the main railway station in New York.

CHAPTER 16 – More on Holden's feelings

1 We learn why Holden admires the nuns.

2 Holden hears a song.

3 He buys a present for his sister and tickets for his date.

Holden thinks about the nuns and tries to imagine his mother or his friends' mothers working for charity. He says they would only do it if it brought them attention and tells us he admires the nuns. Holden's thoughts about the nuns give us more information about his values. The nuns are poor but are doing something which Holden sees as worthwhile and good. He sees rich people's attitudes to charity as a way of drawing attention to themselves. They are doing something good but for the wrong reasons.

Holden goes to buy a record called *Little Shirley Beans* for his sister. On his way to the shop a family is walking in front of him. Their son, a boy of six, is singing a song with the lyrics, 'If a body catch a body, coming through the rye'. When Holden hears this he feels less depressed. The short scene when Holden hears the little boy singing is one of only two places in the novel where the author mentions the title. The other reference is in Chapter 22.

DID YOU KNOW?

The song the child is singing is by a famous Scottish writer – Robert Burns.

After he has bought *Little Shirley Beans* for his sister, Holden decides to phone Jane. He gets through but her mother answers and he puts the phone down, saying he wasn't in the mood to talk to her.

Holden buys tickets to a musical for himself and Sally Hayes. He gives us his views on the theatre and tells us about when his brother

D.B. took him and his sister to see *Hamlet.* He goes on to the park to look for Phoebe but she is not there.

Holden's family and friends

This chapter marks the beginning of a new phase of the story. Holden seems to be trying more and more to make contact with his past. Either through getting in touch with his family or by telling us more about his history.

His meetings with Sally in Chapter 17 and with Carl Luce in Chapter 19 show that he wants normal friendships but somehow they don't work out.

Holden is beginning to think about his family more and more. He knows the likelihood of finding his sister in the park is slim, but something drives him to go there. Holden's mood swings between happiness and depression. This is a sign that he is becoming rather unstable. We are starting to approach Holden's breakdown.

 DID YOU KNOW?

Salinger once said that Holden was modelled on a dead school friend, though no one ever discovered who he was.

He decides to walk across the park to the Museum of Natural History (see map on p. 13) and on his way remembers one of his teachers, Miss Aigletinger, taking his junior class there. He talks about seeing a Columbus exhibition and passing through the room containing American Indian exhibits and models of their activities. The comments about the museum exhibits indicate that Holden likes things to stay as they are. He feels secure knowing that the museum will not change, even though individuals will.

We can compare his thoughts on the museum to the way Holden wants his memories of Jane Gallagher to remain unspoilt, and also with his memories of childhood when Allie was alive. When he reaches the museum, Holden decides he cannot face going in and leaves in a taxi to meet Sally.

CHAPTER 17 – The date with Sally Hayes

① Holden goes out with Sally Hayes.

② The date ends badly.

Holden arrives at the Biltmore, where he meets Sally Hayes. He tells us he feels like marrying her as soon as he sees her, because she looks so pretty. She is pleased when he tells her and they start kissing in the taxi and he tells her that he loves her. We find out how impulsive Holden can be, which is another sign of his immaturity. His desire to marry Sally, just because she looks attractive, demonstrates this side of his character. As he tells her he loves her, he is telling us that his actions are crazy.

DID YOU KNOW?

When Salinger was twenty-two, he was still living with his parents in New York's Park Avenue, and he used to frequent Greenwich Village – then a bohemian quarter – in the evenings.

They go to the show and Holden tells us that it wasn't too bad. He relates the plot, giving his opinions on the quality of the acting. During the interval they go out for a cigarette and Holden comments on the number of 'phonies' there. Sally sees a boy she knows and spends the interval period talking to him instead of Holden. This upsets Holden.

After the show Holden and Sally go ice-skating at Radio City. He tells us they were the worst skaters on the rink and they go and sit

CHECKPOINT 14

Why does Sally
react how she does
to Holden's
suggestions?

down. Sally asks Holden if he will come to her house on Christmas Eve to decorate the Christmas tree. Holden changes the subject and asks Sally if she ever gets fed up. He tells her what he hates about his life but she is not sympathetic. He asks her to run away with him but this frightens her and she tells him he is shouting at her. Even though Sally is not sympathetic to Holden's feelings, he still asks her to run away with him. She thinks his suggestions are ridiculous and says so.

Holden and the 'phonies'

There is more information given in this chapter about the things Holden thinks are phony. Many of the things he 'hates' are based on what he sees as insincerity. He thinks that many people he knows are shallow and false, unlike the nuns.

In many other parts of the book Holden tells us that the society he lives in is false and the idea of him as an outsider is given more weight by the description of his disastrous date with Sally Hayes. She is a settled member of society, quite happy with the world she lives in. However, Holden seems more and more of an outsider and also increasingly desperate to find a solution or a way out of his problems.

For the first time in the novel Holden tries to convey how he really feels to someone of his own age. He tells Sally about a lot of his fears and 'hates', but she cannot understand his problems. Once again, Holden has tried to explain his state of mind and failed. At this point in the novel he does not seem to be able to relate to anyone.

CHECKPOINT 15

Think about other
parts of the novel
where 'escape'
from difficult
situations is
suggested.

Holden tells Sally she is a 'pain in the ass' and she starts crying. He apologises but she is still upset. Eventually he leaves without her.

Holden tells us he doesn't know why he asked Sally to run away with him, saying he wouldn't have taken her even if she had agreed to go. He tells us that paradoxically he meant what he said to her at the time. We discover from Sally's remarks that Holden is shouting and getting excitable, even though he seems unaware of it. This tendency is also mentioned in Chapter 19. It is a sign that Holden finds it hard to control his behaviour.

CHAPTER 18 – Holden sees a film

1 Holden phones Jane Gallagher again.

2 He arranges to meet Carl Luce.

3 He goes to a film and we learn more about D.B.

After Holden leaves the skating-rink he thinks about phoning Jane again. He remembers seeing her at a dance with a boy called Al Pike, whom he did not like. He is puzzled by what girls see in boys like Al. Yet again we see Holden exhibiting jealousy over an episode from his past which involved Jane. Once more, he fails to contact her. We get the feeling that he is not destined to speak to her and that the one person who could help him will not be available.

He phones Jane but there is no reply. He phones an old acquaintance from school, Carl Luce, and arranges to meet him after telling us there are only three people in his address book: Jane, an old teacher called Mr Antolini, and his father at the office.

Holden and the movies

There is more evidence of Holden saying one thing and doing another when he goes to the movies to kill time before meeting Carl. He has told us several times how much he dislikes the movies. Perhaps this could be linked to the fact that his brother went away to work in Hollywood.

Before the film comes on there is a live Christmas show which he dislikes. He explains the plot of the film to us in detail, telling us it was set in wartime, and says it was phony.

DID YOU KNOW?
No film has ever been made of *A Catcher in the Rye*.

CHECK THE BOOK

A Farewell to Arms is a famous book by Ernest Hemingway and is set in the First World War.

After the film, Holden goes to meet Carl Luce. On the way, he thinks about war films and tells us that D.B. was in the Second World War. Holden explains that he would hate being in the army and would rather die than go to war.

Holden's thoughts about the war would have been quite shocking at the time the novel was published, because America was very proud of its army and its role in the war. This is another way in which Holden is rebelling against the values of the society in which he lives.

Chapter 19 – The meeting with Carl Luce

❶ We read a long conversation between Holden and Carl Luce.

❷ It's revealed that Carl once suggested Holden went to a psychiatrist.

Holden is in the Wicker Bar where he has arranged to meet Carl Luce. He tells us that it is full of 'phonies'. As Carl Luce arrives, Holden informs us that he used to be his student adviser and that he and some other boys used to meet in Luce's room to discuss sex. It is significant that Holden chooses to meet his old student adviser. He is looking for help and companionship, but Luce has grown up and changed.

CHECKPOINT 16

Compare Luce's meeting with Holden. Is it like others in the novel?

Luce and Holden have a conversation which mainly revolves around Holden asking questions about Luce's girlfriends. Luce tells Holden he is going out with a Chinese sculptress, which fascinates Holden. Eventually, Luce tells Holden to stop asking questions about her. Holden's conversation with Luce is like many others in the novel; Holden irritates Luce who obviously finds him immature. We also find Luce telling Holden he is shouting. This time, unlike with Sally, Holden admits he talks loudly when he is excited.

The conversation moves on to Holden telling Luce about his sex life, which he explains is terrible. A lot of the conversation is about

Holden's preoccupation with sexual relationships; sexuality is becoming increasingly important to him. He reveals his immaturity by his childish questions. We find out that in the past Luce has suggested to Holden that he see a psychoanalyst. Luce gets up to leave and Holden pleads with him to stay for one more drink. Luce refuses and departs.

DID YOU KNOW?

'Flits' is an old slang term for 'homosexuals'.

Holden is still frightened of being on his own, as we see from the way he asks Luce to stay. Holden does not really know what to do; it is late on Sunday night and he has nowhere to stay.

CHAPTER 20 – A drunken night

❶ **Holden gets drunk and phones Sally Hayes.**

❷ **Phoebe's present is broken.**

❸ **Holden gets more depressed.**

Holden stays in the Wicker Bar, getting more and more drunk. As he sits there he starts pretending he has been shot again. He decides to phone Jane but, again, he says he isn't in the mood and phones Sally Hayes instead.

CHECKPOINT 17

Why does Holden phone Sally?

After speaking to Sally's grandmother, Holden has a drunken conversation with Sally and promises to go to her house on Christmas Eve; Sally tells him he is drunk and that he should go home to bed. Holden regrets phoning her. When Holden phones Sally it seems again that she is a substitute for the person he really wants to talk to. Once more he has tried to communicate with someone at an inappropriate moment.

Holden tries to sober himself up in the washroom by dunking his head in a sink full of water. He has a brief conversation with the piano-player, who also tells him to go home. His conversation with the piano-player is also 'unfriendly'.

Chapter 20 continued

DID YOU KNOW?

Central Park is the largest park in any city.

When he has left the bar, Holden starts crying and tells us he is very depressed and lonely. He decides to go to the park and look for the ducks on the lake. He is worried about where he will sleep.

Holden's lowest point

The events in this chapter mark the low point of Holden's experiences so far in the novel. He has reached the end of his tether! He has no money left, he is cold, drunk and rather frightened.

Holden's feelings at this point are powerfully brought across by the writer. His thoughts of dying, of visiting his brother's grave, and even his drunken play-acting about being shot, are all reinforcing the sense we get of Holden's fears and depression. Notice how all the experiences Holden has had so far are gradually making his mental state worse and worse.

When he gets to the park, Holden drops Phoebe's record and it breaks. This makes him more depressed. He has trouble finding the lake and sits down on a park bench. He imagines what his funeral would be like if he died and feels sorry for his mother and father.

He tells us the only good thing would be that his little sister would not be allowed to go to his funeral because she is too young.

Holden goes on to talk about visiting his brother Allie's grave with his parents and says how much it upset him.

Eventually Holden decides to sneak home and see his sister Phoebe. Holden's decision to go home and see his sister is very risky, in terms of getting caught by his parents. Perhaps Holden wants to 'get caught' but cannot admit it.

CHECKPOINT 18

Try to locate other places in the novel where death is talked about.

Now take a break!

WHO ARE?

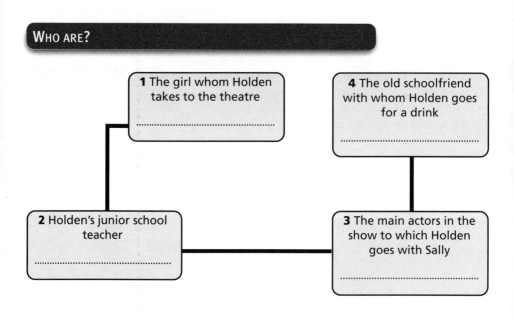

1 The girl whom Holden takes to the theatre

....

4 The old schoolfriend with whom Holden goes for a drink

....

2 Holden's junior school teacher

....

3 The main actors in the show to which Holden goes with Sally

....

LOCATE THE FOLLOWING

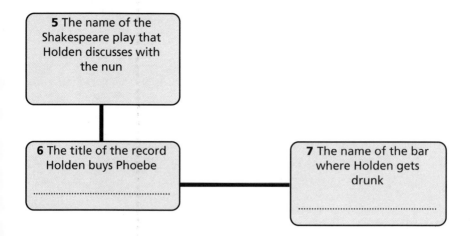

5 The name of the Shakespeare play that Holden discusses with the nun

6 The title of the record Holden buys Phoebe

....

7 The name of the bar where Holden gets drunk

....

Check your answers on p. 98.

CHAPTER 21 – Phoebe and Holden

1 Holden sneaks into his parent's apartment.

2 Phoebe talks to Holden and realises he's been expelled again.

Holden arrives at his parents' apartment and explains that the normal elevator-boy is not on duty. He tells us this will allow him to sneak up and see his sister and leave without his parents knowing. Holden lies to the new elevator-boy, telling him he is going to see the people who live next door to his parents. Holden's talent for lying helps him get into his parents' home. This is one of the only times his lying has a practical purpose; normally he does it just for fun.

After getting into the apartment, Holden goes to his sister's room. He moves slowly and tells us that this is because his mother is a very light sleeper and also has trouble getting to sleep. When he gets to Phoebe's room, he remembers that she sleeps in his brother D.B.'s room when he is away and goes there. Phoebe is asleep so Holden looks through her school notebooks before waking her up. We find out a bit about Holden's home and the family lifestyle. He also seems proud of his sister's schoolbooks. This seems rather strange given that he does not seem interested in his own schoolwork.

Phoebe and Holden start talking; she tells him she is in the school play. He finds out from her that their mother and father are at a party. He relaxes and tells us he doesn't care if they come home and find him there. Holden tells Phoebe about the record and she says that she wants to keep the broken pieces, which amuses Holden.

During their conversation Phoebe suddenly asks Holden why he is home early. She realises he has been thrown out of school again and gets very upset. Holden tries to reassure her, but she keeps repeating that their father will be very angry. He leaves the room to look for some cigarettes.

> **CHECKPOINT 19**
>
> Consider why Holden takes such an interest in his sister's schoolbooks.

Holden's sister

We get a strong impression of Phoebe's character from her conversation with Holden. She obviously cares for her brother. Her distress when she realises he has been thrown out of school is caused by her understanding that there will be resulting family arguments.

During Holden's conversation with Phoebe we see that his younger sister is disappointed in him. Holden thinks that Phoebe will understand his feelings, but she is baffled by his behaviour.

Phoebe is the only one of Holden's family who is actually present in the novel (apart from a very brief appearance of Holden's mother, although she doesn't realise Holden is there). The others are all talked about by Holden. Phoebe's importance is developed through the rest of the novel and the novel ends with Holden looking at Phoebe on the carrousel.

CHAPTER 22 – 'The Catcher in the Rye'

❶ Holden has a long conversation with Phoebe.

❷ He remembers James Castle.

❸ He talks about being 'a catcher in the rye'.

DID YOU KNOW?

'Veteran's Day' is the American expression for a 'school reunion'.

Holden goes back into the room to see Phoebe. She continues to ignore him and it reminds him of when the fencing team ignored him on his last day at Pencey Prep. Phoebe is still preoccupied with Holden being thrown out of school. Eventually Holden tries to explain to Phoebe why he did not like Pencey. He tells her it was full of phonies and mentions briefly how badly Ackley was treated there. He remembers Spencer and accuses him of sucking up to the headmaster and describes 'Veterans' Day'.

Phoebe tells Holden that he doesn't like anything and asks him to name something he does like. Holden tells us he can't concentrate and that the only thing he could remember were the nuns and an incident at Elkton Hills, one of his old schools, where a boy jumped out of a window to his death rather than give in to some bullies. James Castle will form an important link with Mr Antolini, a teacher whom Holden respects and turns to for answers to his problems. By mentioning Ackley and James Castle, the boy who died at Elkton Hills, the author reinforces our image of Holden as an outsider.

His mind is filled with images of unwanted people during his talk with Phoebe. The things he 'likes' or, in other words, thinks are morally good, are not valued by society; examples are the nuns and the boy who dies rather than take back what he has said. Instead of telling Phoebe this, he tells her he likes Allie.

Phoebe continues to probe Holden about what he wants to be in life. Holden dismisses his sister's suggestions and goes on to ask her if she knows the song *If a body catch a body comin' through the rye*. She tells him it's a poem by Robert Burns and that it is 'meet' not 'catch'. Holden then describes to her an image in his mind of himself standing on the edge of a cliff, stopping children who are running out of a field of rye from falling over the edge. He says he would be '*The catcher in the rye*'.

DID YOU KNOW?

When *The Catcher in the Rye* was first published, critics called it 'daring', 'obscene' and 'blasphemous'

Catcher in the Rye

This is the only time in the novel the complete title, *The Catcher in the Rye*, is mentioned. Holden's explanation of what he would like to be is completely unrealistic. But when we look beneath the surface of his description it seems to give us Holden's real dream. He wants to save others from what has happened to him. He feels that he has, in one way, 'fallen off a cliff'. He wants to protect children like Allie, Ackley and James Castle from the world. It is significant that it is during his conversation with Phoebe that this comes up. She represents hope for Holden, just as the little boy does whom we met in Chapter 16.

Holden decides to phone his old English teacher from Elkton Hills, Mr Antolini. He leaves the room, telling Phoebe to stay awake.

CHAPTER 23 – An evening with Phoebe

❶ **Holden arranges to visit Mr Antolini.**

❷ **Holden hides from his mother.**

❸ **He leaves the family apartment.**

CHECKPOINT 20

Notice the contradiction in Holden's behaviour in this chapter.

Holden phones Mr Antolini and arranges to go and see him straight away. Holden reveals to us that Mr Antolini was the person who finally picked up the dead boy, James Castle, at Elkton Hills school. Holden's remarks about Mr Antolini give us a clue about why he wants to see him. He is a figure of authority whom Holden thinks will help him. Mr Antolini is portrayed as a caring person who does not think about himself when helping others. This quality is similar to the nuns whom Holden admires.

When Holden has returned to D.B.'s room, he dances to the music on the radio with Phoebe. He tells us that Phoebe is a good dancer. Holden sits down on the bed and tells us he is breathless, due to the number of cigarettes he has been smoking.

They hear the front door open and realise that their parents have returned home, so Holden hides in the wardrobe. Phoebe and her mother have a conversation, which involves Phoebe covering up for the smell of smoke created by Holden, and Holden is not noticed. Their mother leaves the room, saying goodnight to Phoebe.

EXAMINER'S SECRET

Using the correct literary terms will improve your grade. Here you could note the **symbolism** of Holden giving his hat to his sister.

Holden borrows Phoebe's Christmas savings and tells her he won't go away until after her school play. He suddenly starts to cry and Phoebe tries to comfort him. Holden tells us he cried for a long time but finally gets his coat and gets ready to leave. Before he goes he gives Phoebe his red hunting hat.

When Holden breaks down in tears this is a sign that he feels he is letting his sister down. He feels that he has to run away and yet he is frightened of leaving the person he cares most about. Phoebe's willingness to give him her Christmas savings and the way she deceives her mother for him makes him realise he is going away from someone who genuinely cares about him.

CHAPTER 24 – An upsetting encounter

❶ Mr Antolini and Holden have a long conversation.

❷ Holden is upset by Mr Antolini.

Holden arrives at Mr Antolini's house, telling us that he knew Mr Antolini well and explaining that he used to come and see Holden quite often.

Mr Antolini and Holden begin a long conversation. This is one of the longest conversations Holden has with someone in the whole novel. It is one of the only times Holden seems to be able to talk freely with someone. However, he does not feel well and it seems difficult for him to concentrate on what Mr Antolini is saying. Mr Antolini asks Holden why he got expelled from Pencey, but Holden talks about why he failed the Oral Expression part of his English course. He also comments quite frequently about Mr Antolini's drinking, making him appear not quite as stable and reliable as his conversation indicates.

Mrs Antolini comes in with coffee and says she is going to bed. After she has gone Mr Antolini tells Holden that he had lunch with his father and that they were both very worried about him. He says he feels that Holden is going to fail in life unless he starts to think about what he really wants to be and then applies himself to his studies.

Mr Antolini continues talking, trying to explain what he thinks Holden is going through. During the conversation Holden has told us he feels tired, and when he yawns Mr Antolini says he will make

DID YOU KNOW?

'Pencey Prep' was based on Forge Military Academy where Salinger attended from the age of fifteen.

up a bed for him on the couch. Whilst he is getting it ready he asks Holden about Sally Hayes and Jane Gallagher. Holden says he will ring Jane tomorrow.

DID YOU KNOW?

The Catcher in the Rye was written at a time when homosexuality was illegal and rarely discussed openly.

There is a genuine feeling that Mr Antolini cares for Holden and is concerned about his future. He wants to work out what Holden is going through and we feel that he is the first person we have come across who comes close to understanding Holden's predicament.

Holden goes to sleep but suddenly wakes up to find Mr Antolini patting his head. Holden becomes very disturbed by this and decides to leave Mr Antolini's house.

> **Another let-down**
>
> The shock that Holden feels when he wakes up, and his reaction, seem extreme. He feels that Mr Antolini is making sexual advances to him. He says that Mr Antolini was behaving like a 'pervert'.
>
> Holden's perception of what has happened is that someone whom he respected and trusted has let him down. This incident is, in some ways, the final straw for Holden. The last person Holden turns to for advice and help seems to care about him for all the wrong reasons, as far as Holden is concerned. This connects to other parts of the book where Holden is disappointed by adult behaviour. All through the novel Holden's experiences of 'adult' life show it to be either corrupt or false.

Whilst he is waiting for the lift, he has an uncomfortable conversation with Mr Antolini. At the end of the chapter Holden is out on the streets again and we feel that he is cast adrift from everyone he knows. The writer has created a real sense of foreboding for us.

CHAPTER 25 – The climax of Holden's tale

1 **Holden wanders the streets of New York.**

2 **He visits the museum.**

3 **Phoebe rides on a carrousel.**

It is dawn on Monday as Holden leaves Mr Antolini's house. He goes to Grand Central Station (see map on p. 13) and sleeps on a bench until about nine o'clock. He reflects on what happened at Mr Antolini's and thinks that, perhaps, he should have returned to the house.

Holden wanders around the streets and tells us he was looking around for the two nuns he talked to the day before. Suddenly Holden has a frightening psychological experience: he keeps thinking he is going to disappear. To overcome his fear, he pretends to talk to Allie.

When Holden has recovered from the experience, he decides to go away, to hitchhike to the far west of the country. He gets excited about his journey and decides to go and arrange to meet Phoebe at

 DID YOU KNOW?
'Carrousel' is a French spelling, and the merry-go-round as we know it originated in France in the late seventeenth century.

the Museum of Art before he leaves, to return her money and say goodbye.

After leaving her a note he thinks about phoning Jane Gallagher but informs us he isn't in the mood. He goes to the museum. While waiting for Phoebe two small boys ask him if he knows where the Egyptian section of the museum is. Holden starts telling them about Egyptian mummies. The boys leave and Holden goes to see the mummies. By mentioning the mummies in the museum, the writer cleverly links the early part of Holden's tale with what is happening to him now. We recall Holden's failure in his History exam, part of the reason for being thrown out of Pencey and, therefore, part of the reason for his current plight. Holden then goes to the toilet, telling us he feels ill. He passes out briefly but recovers.

Holden goes back to the museum entrance and sees Phoebe across the street. She is carrying a large suitcase and, when they meet, tells Holden she is going away with him. Holden is shocked and tells his sister she cannot go. Phoebe starts to cry and Holden tells her he isn't going anywhere; he offers to walk her back to school but she tells him she isn't going.

> **CHECKPOINT 21**
>
> Think of other clues through the novel that Holden is physically ill.

On the verge of breakdown

In this chapter we have reached the climax of the story Holden wants to tell. He is physically exhausted, ill and unable to think straight. He has nowhere to go and his plan to go away to the 'wild west' is as unrealistic as his desire to be 'the catcher in the rye'. There is an increasing sense of desperation surrounding Holden's thoughts and actions.

Eventually Holden realises that he has to take some kind of responsibility when Phoebe insists on going away with him. He has learnt the lesson that what a person does always has consequences. He knows that he wants his sister to be happy and we feel that he cares for her more than for anyone else in the novel. He cannot even think about her accompanying him and therefore makes the decision not to go. His love for his sister has overcome his fear of facing his parents and it is perhaps this realisation that makes him so happy at the end.

Instead of returning Phoebe to school, Holden takes her to the zoo. They leave the zoo and Holden takes Phoebe to the park where there is a carrousel. Phoebe rides on the carrousel, putting Holden's hat back on his head before she gets on. As Holden watches Phoebe on the carrousel it starts to rain. He suddenly feels deliriously happy and says he doesn't know why. He just enjoys watching Phoebe on the carrousel.

? DID YOU KNOW?
A carrousel is a fairground merry-go-round.

CHAPTER 26 – More from the hospital bed

1 Holden tells us he's finished what he wants to tell us.

2 We find out he's going back to school.

Holden informs us that he has told us as much as he wants to. He hints at what has happened to him since being in the park with Phoebe, saying he went home, became sick and was eventually put in the place from where he has narrated the story.

Chapter 26 continued

DID YOU KNOW?

'Fall' is the American word for 'autumn'.

Holden tells us that he is going back to school in September, but is still unsure how he will behave when he gets there. He says he will try to apply himself.

He tells us that his brother, D.B., comes to visit him and has asked Holden what he feels about the story he has told. Holden says he doesn't know, but that he misses all the people he has talked about.

> **Back to the beginning**
>
> This final short chapter rounds off the novel. In some ways it is like the first page of Chapter 1, 'returning' the reader to the hospital that Holden is in. We feel a sense of relief that Holden is on the way to overcoming his problems, but there is also a feeling that there could still be trouble ahead for him.

Now take a break!

WHO ARE?

1 The boy who died at Elkton Hills

....

2 The character Phoebe is to play in the school pageant

....

LOCATE THE FOLLOWING

3 Where Holden's parents are when he returns home

....

7 Where Holden and Phoebe go when they meet in Chapter 25

....

4 The name of the poet who wrote, *If a body meet a body coming through the rye*

....

6 Where Holden goes after leaving Mr Antolini's

....

5 What Mr Antolini drinks

....

Check your answers on p. 98.

PART THREE

COMMENTARY

THEMES

All the main themes in *The Catcher in the Rye* link to Holden's personal experience of the world.

However, we can isolate four major themes in the novel. These are:

- Relationships
- The individual and society
- The effects of the environment
- Innocence and childhood

These themes interlink to influence and develop the overall story of Holden's search for an answer to his troubles and his descent into psychological breakdown.

CHECK THE BOOK

Albert Camus' *The Outsider* (1942) was the first modern novel to portray this feeling of alienation from society.

CHECK THE BOOK

Look at Barry Hines' *A Kestrel for a Knave* and see if there are similarities in its sense of alienation.

RELATIONSHIPS

Holden as an outsider

One of the main strands of the novel concerns Holden's problems in forming relationships. In many parts of the novel we find Holden telling us how lonely he feels; this is shown by his increasingly desperate attempts to befriend people. From the beginning of his story he has problems getting on with others.

School

We first meet him when he has been 'ostracised' by the fencing team. He is on his own when everyone else is enjoying themselves at a football match. His relationships with his schoolfriends are insecure: he talks to Ackley but tells us he doesn't like him; he admires Stradlater in some ways but ends up fighting with him and leaving Pencey.

Adults and parents

The first adult we meet, Mr Spencer, cannot understand Holden, even though he seems to like him. The other important adult figure, Mr Antolini, also cannot understand Holden. Even though he tries to give Holden advice about his life, Holden just feels tired and cannot really relate to what is being said to him. Holden's relationship with his parents seems distant, as if he thinks they do not really care about him. Holden's problems are mainly caused by his and his parents' inability to form a family relationship of trust and understanding.

Meaningful conversations

All through the novel Holden attempts to engage people of all sorts in conversation, but his only meaningful ones are with the two nuns and his younger sister Phoebe. Here he is being himself. Many of his other attempts at talking to others are characterised by him lying or pretending to be someone he is not. He lies to Mrs Morrow on the train and tries to be sophisticated with the three girls he meets in the Edmont Hotel. In New York he attempts to relate to people in what he sees as an adult way but fails again.

Relationships in the past

Holden tends to remember his relationships with people in his past more favourably. He speaks fondly of how he and his brothers were happy together as children. When he talks about his brother Allie we sense a closeness which is not there in his present life.

His other really significant relationship was with Jane Gallagher when they spent one summer together. In a way this is the closest Holden has come to being in love. His failure to contact Jane when he is in New York shows how he cannot relate to anyone. He is frightened of spoiling the memory of a good relationship and substitutes Sally Hayes for her, though he feels she is shallow. He cannot relate to Sally and their brief day out ends in another failed relationship for Holden.

He often talks about sex and mistakenly believes that this aspect of a relationship is the most 'adult' or important. This is a typical

DID YOU KNOW?
One critic, Arthur Mizener, described Salinger's novel as 'always hovering in ambivalence between comedy and tragedy'

response for a boy of his age. Holden's inability to understand sexuality shows his immaturity.

THE INDIVIDUAL AND SOCIETY

Society and materialism

 CHECK
THE FILM
Jerry Maguire starring Tom Cruise deals with a someone working in the movies who feels that he is phony.

Much of Holden's story concerns his reactions to the values of the society in which he lives. He is disillusioned with his world and rebels against it. The society he lives in seems to him to be shallow and only concerned with material things; money is the most important thing and Holden feels this is wrong.

This can be seen by the fact that the only two adults Holden feels empathy with are the nuns. Nuns have to give up material things and money; they take vows of poverty. They seem to Holden to be the only people he meets who genuinely care about others.

The values of school

Holden's dislike of his society's values can be clearly seen at Pencey, where he is very sarcastic about the school and its claims to 'mould' students into valuable members of society. School is normally where young people learn to become responsible members of their society, but Holden rejects the 'values' of Pencey just as he did the other schools from which he was expelled. Holden mocks Mr Ossenburger, someone who became rich after leaving Pencey, and says he is only regarded as important because of his wealth, rather than because he has done anything of value for others. All the schools Holden has attended are for the rich and privileged. Many members of society would think themselves lucky to have these opportunities, but Holden seems to feel guilt and anger at his situation and rebels against it.

New York people

The social and moral values of the people Holden meets in New York are portrayed as either corrupt or petty and snobbish. The places Holden goes to in search of companionship are full of people only interested in themselves and how others see them. The piano-player at Ernie's bar and the couple whom he meets there are examples of this.

The prostitute and the elevator-man are examples of how corrupt society has become. In one of Holden's 'weak' moments he thinks he can buy the company and the experience he wants, but when he behaves as he thinks other adult men in his society behave this results in embarrassment and humiliation.

Pressure to conform

Throughout the novel Holden is critical of the society in which he lives. No aspects of it seem worthwhile. The pressure which society puts on people to conform and be like one another puts an enormous strain on Holden. He is portrayed as an outsider who tries to fit in but cannot. This is the dilemma for Holden that leads to his breakdown.

THE EFFECTS OF THE ENVIRONMENT

The idea of environment affecting someone's behaviour is an important theme of *The Catcher in the Rye*. Holden moves through three main environments: Pencey Prep, the clubs, bars and streets of New York City (see map on p. 13) and lastly Central Park. They all have an impact on him and he tries to escape from all of these places at one time or another in the story.

Pencey Prep

At Pencey Holden is a part of the community, although he is on the verge of leaving. He deals with the people he comes into contact with on an equal basis. He is secure and confident at the school even though he tells us he does not like it and the environment there seems to stifle him. Holden views the school as boring, trivial and phony. Although it is his fight with Stradlater which finally makes him leave, we often feel Holden wants to escape from the confines of school. Holden cannot obey the rules and regulations which govern the boarding school environment.

New York

J.D. Salinger often makes the streets of New York seem a frightening place. One example of this is his description at the beginning of Chapter 12; another, in Chapter 25, is when Holden feels he is disappearing and that the city is going to 'swallow' him

DID YOU KNOW?
The critic, Arthur Mizener, wrote of *The Catcher in the Rye* that 'a great deal of his most brilliant wit ... is close to desperation'

up. He will become one of the casualties of his environment, like many other city-dwellers.

Central Park

The park represents one place where Holden can find some happiness and it is here that his story ends. However, the park is also a frightening place for him and it is his fears in the park which lead to him going home at the end of Chapter 20. The park is still the place where Holden can be happy with his sister, perhaps because it has associations for him with his childhood, a more innocent and happy time.

Effect on emotions

The different environments in which Holden finds himself all contribute to his inner emotions:

DID YOU KNOW?
At the time this novel was written, it would have been even more daring for a teenager to enter a bar or see a prostitute.

- The museums and the park make him nostalgic and he wishes that time could stand still or even go backwards

- The clubs and bars bring out Holden's cynicism but also his insecurities and naivety

- The city as a whole brings on Holden's depression

- The pace and confusion of city life reflect Holden's own confusion and fear

INNOCENCE AND CHILDHOOD

Transition

In *The Catcher in the Rye* Holden is at the age between childhood and adulthood. The difficulties he has making this transition are a principal part of the story; it is a type of story called a **bildungsroman**, but not a conventional one. Holden's development is twisted and he does not reach maturity by the end of the story. We also only find out about his earlier life in **flashbacks**.

In some ways Holden is afraid of growing up. He seems unable to face the responsibilities which come as he gets older. This is shown by his continued 'flunking' of his exams, even though he is obviously intelligent. His answer to his problems is a typically childlike dream, to 'run away' and have an adventure: he runs away from Pencey Prep and later talks to Sally Hayes and his sister Phoebe about escaping to the country.

Allie and Jane

Holden's happiest memories concern his own childhood before the death of his brother Allie. The only other time he has seemed genuinely happy since then is the time he spent with Jane Gallagher. These relationships were innocent ones, they happened before Holden saw how cruel the world could be. When his brother died, Holden's own childhood was lost and he had to confront something he did not understand; his reaction is extreme and marks the beginning of his problems.

His relationship with Jane was innocent. Even though they kissed, Holden informs us it wasn't on the mouth! They played games together, like draughts and golf. Holden does not want to let these happy memories go and he idealises his time with Jane. His reluctance to phone her reinforces the sense that he does not want to see Jane grown-up: his childhood memory would be shattered. This is also clearly seen when Holden fights Stradlater and becomes almost obsessive about what Stradlater may have done with Jane. He is afraid that, because of Stradlater, Jane may have lost a part of her 'innocence' and moved into the adult world.

Holden's childlike qualities

Holden's innocence and childlike qualities are exposed when he tries to act out his perceptions of adult behaviour. They all end in disaster or depression. His initial attempts to get alcohol are thwarted and when he does get served he gets drunk and breaks his sister's present. His experience with the prostitute shows his innocence regarding sex, while she provides a contrast to this innocence. She is roughly the same age as Holden and her life is already corrupted by the world in which she lives. His rounds of the clubs and bars all leave him depressed.

 DID YOU KNOW?

At Forge Military Academy, Salinger got so drunk one night that a fellow pupil had to knock him out to stop him waking up the militia.

Fantasy and reality

Holden's tendency to fantasise also emphasises his childlike behaviour. He often retreats to the world of the imagination when things in the real world become too much for him. Examples of this are when he pretends to be shot and his great love for books and stories. His fantasies of life in the Far West, or in the mountains with Sally Hayes, show he is unable to face reality and that he still has the unrealistic dreams of a young adolescent. Holden's admissions that he doesn't understand women and adults in general contribute to our view of him as immature.

Holden's quest completed

Holden cares about the innocent aspects of his world, which have not changed as he is growing up: the park, the children's zoo and the museums he visited. His sister Phoebe, still uncorrupted by the adult world, is the only person to whom he can really relate. It is the innocent **image** of his sister on a children's fairground ride which finally makes him feel happy for a moment. Holden's quest is complete; he seeks refuge in the innocent pleasure of a merry-go-round, rather than the adult world he has inhabited over the previous two days.

STRUCTURE

NARRATIVE STRUCTURE

CHECK THE BOOK

Chaucer's *Canterbury Tales* also use a frame narrative device. The individual tales of the pilgrims are framed by Chaucer's story about their pilgrimage.

The Catcher in the Rye is a story told within a frame. The story is of the three days of Holden's life between leaving Pencey Prep and going home to his parents, on to a therapist or doctor of some kind in a hospital in California. This **frame narrative** is contained within the first page of Chapter 1 and the last chapter.

The core of the story concerns what happened to Holden in New York, but this story also contains many **flashbacks** to his childhood and to other events in his past. The novel is essentially **episodic**; it does not have a traditional 'beginning, middle and end' and progress strictly in an even time-sequence. Instead it relates various significant episodes in Holden's past and present life, sometimes jumping backwards and forwards, in order to build a detailed picture of a disturbed and confused young man who is heading towards emotional breakdown. There is, however, a definite structure to the novel.

The structure of *The Catcher in the Rye* is formed by four main sections as reflected in the **Summaries**. Each section has a climax which moves on the action and also reveals more about Holden's character and feelings.

Leaving Pencey Prep

The climax in the first section is Holden's fight with Stradlater, which drives Holden to leave school earlier than he had to. We also realise at the end of this section that there are people about whom Holden cares deeply, for example his dead brother Allie and Jane Gallagher.

The Edmont Hotel

In the second section we have the disastrous climax to Holden's attempts at acting as a suave, young man on the town. This is his encounter with the prostitute and occurs almost exactly in the middle of the novel. It is a powerful episode, which makes Holden leave the hotel and also shows his vulnerability to the harsh, corrupt world of the city. At this point we also get a sense of how depressed and insecure Holden feels and we sense that something terrible will possibly happen to him.

Faces from the past

At the end of the third section, Holden has reached his lowest point and he returns home. This is a turning point in the story. Holden is frightened and alone, and, despite his efforts through this section to befriend people, he ends up drunk and alone in Central Park, looking for the ducks which Salinger uses as a **symbol** of escape. Holden's problems in finding the lake are a device to show he has no escape-routes left. He has no options left but to return to his home.

DID YOU KNOW?
Stradlater is based on Salinger's real-life friend and room mate at Forge Military Academy.

Reunited with Phoebe

The end of the main tale is mysterious. The sudden ending with
Holden's happiness at seeing Phoebe on the carrousel leaves us
wondering about what happened to Holden when he returned
home. The writer does not provide us with a **closure** where the
plight of the **protagonist** is resolved. We have to form our own
opinion of what happened next. The novel ends with us wondering
if there will be a sequel, even though in the last chapter Holden says
he wishes he hadn't started telling his story.

**DID YOU
KNOW?**
The structure of the
novel itself may be
described as
'circular' too, as it
ends at the same
time and place at
which it began.

INTERNAL STRUCTURE

Although J.D. Salinger does not make extensive use of symbols,
significant symbols are used to link important themes and ideas
within the novel. For instance there are many circular objects which
are associated with comfort, happiness and completion for Holden:
the roundabout, the gold ring, Phoebe's record and Holden's red
hunting hat (which also symbolises his individuality). Allie's
baseball mitt is a relic of the past. Even certain characters represent
specific values: for instance Jane symbolises purity and the
untouchable innocence of childhood (see **Innocence and childhood**
in **Themes**). Such use of symbols indicates how carefully *The
Catcher in the Rye* has been structured.

CHARACTERS

It is impossible to give a description of every single person
mentioned in the novel. Just as in real life, Holden has many chance
meetings with people who are not that important to the novel as a
whole, but who serve to increase the sense of real experiences (as in
realism) we get when reading *The Catcher in the Rye*. The
characters described here all have an important impact on the story.

THE CAULFIELD FAMILY

Holden Caulfield

Holden is the main character in the novel and we see the world
through his eyes. He is a young man aged sixteen at the time of the

events he describes to us, an adolescent on the verge of adulthood. Holden's language is meant to be typical of a teenager of the era and this defines his character for us (see **Language and style**). He comes across as a witty individual who, nevertheless, can be irritating to those around him. He is from a stable background and his parents are quite wealthy; they live in an expensive part of New York. He has a younger sister and two brothers, one of whom is dead.

During the course of the novel we discover more and more about Holden's past and realise that he is a troubled young man. He is confused about much of the world around him and he is disillusioned with life. His sense of unhappiness and depression increases as the novel progresses, until he has a breakdown. It is left to the reader to decide whether this is because Holden is a 'weak' character or because he has experienced intolerable pressures and no one has helped him to deal with them.

Witty
Sarcastic
Emotionally disturbed
Disillusioned
Dissatisfied with life

We are shown that Holden has a strong sense of moral values which often clashes with those of people around him. When he does things he knows are wrong he feels immediately guilty; all through the novel there is a sense of Holden's guilt about his behaviour and this is one of the main reasons he is afraid to go home to his parents.

Holden has a vivid imagination and a love of books and stories in general. Even though he claims to hate the movies, he spends quite a lot of time pretending to be in them! This frequent contradiction of himself is another of Holden's character traits. He tries to behave like an adult by smoking and drinking, going out with girls and hanging around in bars, but he is highly critical of others whom he sees living such a lifestyle and still yearns for his innocent childhood.

Phoebe Caulfield

Holden's ten-year-old younger sister is described by Holden as pretty, skinny and having red hair. Phoebe likes going to the movies and can tell a good film from a bad one. She is an intelligent girl with an inquisitive nature and has a love for writing stories. She seems to enjoy school and has lots of notebooks. Holden says she is

Pretty
Intelligent
Stubborn
Inquisitive
Loyal to Holden

**CHECK
THE BOOK**

George Eliot's *The Mill on the Floss* relates the intense relationship between another sister and brother, Maggie Gulliver and her brother Tom.

a neat and tidy person and she seems very organised and 'grown up' for her age.

Phoebe becomes a very important character towards the end of the novel. For Holden she represents innocence and goodness and is a reminder of when life was happy at home. She is the main reason for Holden eventually going home. Phoebe becomes very distressed when she finds out that Holden has been expelled and this shows that she cares deeply about him. When he decides to go away, Phoebe insists on going with him. This also demonstrates the stubborn side of her nature. She is portrayed as a wise child, but one who still behaves in the manner which we would expect of a ten-year-old.

Allie Caulfield

Allie was Holden's younger brother by two years, who died when Holden was thirteen. Holden describes Allie as a popular and sensitive boy. Although he is not often mentioned he is an important character as his death could be what sparked off Holden's problems.

D.B. Caulfield

Holden's elder brother D.B. is a writer. He moved to Hollywood to write for the film industry, which Holden feels is a waste of his talent. He visits Holden at the hospital in California, where Holden is recovering as he tells his story.

Holden's mother and father

Holden's mother is mentioned briefly and is described as being highly strung, especially since the death of Allie. Holden's father is also only referred to in passing; he is a corporate lawyer who earns a high salary. Although they are discussed very little, they are important to the novel as it is Holden's guilt and fear of their reaction that prevents him from going home.

SCHOOLFRIENDS AND CONTEMPORARIES

Robert Ackley

'Ackley boy', as Holden calls him, is an important character early in the novel. He has the room next door to Holden at Pencey Prep. He is described as an unpopular boy. He is a senior pupil, but no one seems close to him. He has acne and bad teeth and is a 'slob'. Holden tells us he was not liked by anyone, including himself, and he was prevented from joining various societies set up by the other boys. He is an outsider in many ways, just like Holden, but for different reasons.

Outsider
Irritating
Ugly
Unpopular
Lonely

Although Holden spends a good deal of time telling us about Ackley's bad qualities, he is the last person Holden goes to see before leaving Pencey. Holden seems to realise that Ackley, like himself, has no one with whom to identify. Ackley often tries to start conversations or make friendships with people but is shunned, just like Holden in New York.

Ward Stradlater

Stradlater is another character who is important at the beginning of the novel. He is Holden's roommate and his senior. He is described by Holden as handsome and popular with the girls, someone who knows about the world and is sexually active. He has seduced girls in the past and Holden thinks he is one of the few students he knows who has actually had sex. Stradlater is portrayed as the 'model' for society's idea of what a young man of his age should be like. He has his faults but, by and large, his behaviour is that of a 'normal', well-balanced, American male of his particular era. The way Stradlater is represented allows us to contrast him with Holden and sharpens our sense of Holden being an outsider, unable to behave as society dictates.

Worldly wise
Sophisticated
Well built
Popular with girls
Mature?

He is particularly important in the novel because he is the person who causes Holden to leave Pencey early. Stradlater seems to be able to do the things that Holden wants to do but cannot. There is a feeling throughout the novel that Stradlater makes Holden jealous, particularly his relationship with Jane Gallagher.

Sensitive
Innocent
Beautiful

Jane Gallagher

Although we never meet Jane in the novel she is a major character, as she occupies so much of Holden's thoughts. She is a sensitive girl with whom Holden spent a summer holiday two years before the action of the novel takes place. She is portrayed by Holden as his perfect companion and one of the few people with whom he has ever felt comfortable.

Jane is, indirectly, another reason for Holden leaving Pencey. He fights with Stradlater because he believes he has behaved badly with Jane. Throughout the novel Holden thinks of phoning her, but never gets to speak to her. It is as if she represents a beautiful memory for Holden which he is afraid of spoiling, so he is unable to talk to her.

Edgar Marsalla

A boy who causes a disturbance at Pencey by farting in a speech.

Carl Luce

Holden's old student adviser at Whooton school. He meets Holden for drinks and we realise that Luce has become an adult who does not want to respond to Holden's immature questions.

James Castle

The boy who died at Elkton Hills School. He jumped out of a window rather than take back something he believed to be true. He is an important link between Holden and Mr Antolini.

Sally Hayes

One of Holden's old girlfriends whom he takes out one afternoon in New York. She is described as very attractive but shallow. She comes from a wealthy background and is happy with her life. Holden upsets her by calling her 'a pain in the ass' when she refuses to run away with him.

Sunny

The prostitute who comes to Holden's room at the Edmont Hotel. A young woman the same age as Holden.

AUTHORITY FIGURES

Mr Spencer

Holden's History teacher at Pencey Prep. An old man who was friendly towards his students, often inviting them into his home for hot drinks. When we meet him he is suffering from flu and Holden wishes he hadn't come to see him. He shows concern for Holden and cannot understand why he is failing so badly at school.

The main scene involving Mr Spencer is when he reads Holden's History exam paper to him, showing up its inadequacies. Holden feels that Mr Spencer is being sarcastic, but tells us that Mr Spencer felt badly about failing him in the exam.

Mr Spencer is important to the novel as he is the first 'adult' we meet. He typifies the 'generation gap' and is one of many 'grown-ups' in the novel whom Holden wishes he hadn't started talking to! Although he is kind and caring, he cannot relate to Holden's feelings.

Elderly
Concerned

Mr Antolini

Mr Antolini is Holden's ex-English teacher from Elkton Hills school, described as the best teacher he ever had. A youngish man, not much older than Holden's brother D.B., Mr Antolini is married to an older woman. They live in an expensive apartment in New York and are friendly with the Caulfield family. He makes an impression on Holden by being the person who goes to pick up the body of the boy, James Castle, who killed himself at Elkton Hills.

Mr Antolini is the last person Holden goes to in his quest to find someone to understand and help him and who can relate to him. They have a long conversation, during which Mr Antolini is described as drinking quite heavily. Mr Antolini tries to get through to Holden that he may fail in life if he does not pull himself together and decide what he wants. He shows genuine concern for Holden and we feel he really cares.

Intelligent
Friendly
Concerned
Near-alcoholic

When Holden goes to sleep at the Antolini's apartment he is woken up by Mr Antolini ruffling his hair; this is interpreted by Holden as a sexual advance and the last character Holden looks up to comes under suspicion for having false motives.

The nuns

CHECK THE NET
Search for the names of the main characters to read more about them.

Two nuns whom Holden meets in a station cafeteria. They are also teachers, one of them an English teacher. Holden has one of his few successful conversations with them and thinks about them periodically after their meeting.

Miss Aigletinger

One of Holden's old junior school teachers, who used to take them to the museums around Central Park.

Mr Thurmer

The headmaster of Pencey Prep.

Mrs Morrow

The mother of one of the boys Holden knew at Pencey. Holden has a conversation on the train with her, telling outrageous lies about what his schoolfriends think of her son Ernest.

Maurice

The elevator-man with whom Holden makes the arrangement to see the prostitute. He beats up Holden after a row about the money owed to the prostitute.

LANGUAGE AND STYLE

NARRATIVE STYLE

The particular style of writing used by J.D. Salinger is crucial to *The Catcher in the Rye*. The novel is written entirely from Holden's **point of view.**

We are asked to believe that Holden is telling his story to a doctor or a counsellor of some kind and therefore it is important that the language sounds like spoken English. Salinger uses a number of techniques to achieve this effect.

Spoken language features

The writer uses **first person narration** – Salinger uses the first person pronoun 'I' throughout the story and this helps to bring Holden's character alive. He also uses what is known as 'direct address' at the beginning of the story. This is where the narrator uses the pronoun 'you'. This makes readers feel that they are being spoken to personally. It is how we would talk to someone if we were telling them about something that had happened to us.

Holden's 'voice'

Holden has many 'stock phrases', which are repeated throughout the novel to give an impression of a particular individual's speech style. This gives the feeling that it is someone actually talking. The style is what we might call informal language. Holden has many habitual phrases. He often uses the expression 'it really was' or 'I really was', as if he wants us to believe him but is afraid that we will not. His other main phrase is 'that kills me', usually used to indicate that something really amuses him. These and other expressions like 'phony' make Holden an individual with his own way of speaking, but they also echo the slang of the time.

CHECK THE BOOK
Jonathan Green's *Dictionary of Slang* explains many of the slang words used by Holden.

He frequently strays from the subject, as a person would when telling a story to a friend. These are called 'digressions'. Holden jumps to a seemingly unrelated story because something he has told us has reminded him of another incident in his life – for example, when he tells us about Mrs Aigletinger in Chapter 16. Another way this technique is used is when Holden explains his relationships with the characters he mentioned – as in his long explanation to Stradlater about how he knew Jane Gallagher. This sometimes creates the impression that the novel has not been carefully structured, but this is probably the author's intention and adds to the sense of **realism**.

Swear words

One of the first things we notice about Holden's use of language is his use of swear words; although today they seem mild, at the time they would have been quite shocking. He uses the word 'crap' quite frequently and expressions like 'my ass'. He has a limited set of insults such as 'you sonovabitch' and 'you moron'. He often uses the work 'bastard', either to describe how he feels 'I was ... like a bastard' or to describe someone else, as in 'witty bastard'. Again this creates the feeling of a real spoken voice.

Holden does not like certain swear words though and spends time at the end of the story rubbing off graffiti, saying 'fuck you', from the walls of his sister's school. This attitude towards swear words creates the impression that Holden has certain morals about language. He undersatnds that certain language should not be used in front of some people.

DID YOU KNOW?

One critic, Donald P. Costello, forecast in the 1950s that 'in the coming decades, *The Catcher in the Rye* will be studied ... as an example of teenage vernacular in the 1950s. The book will be a significant historical record of a type of speech rarely made available in permanent form'.

Exaggeration

Another characteristic feature of Holden's language is his tendency to exaggerate. There are many instances of this in the novel and this is the main way in which J.D. Salinger portrays the humorous side of Holden's character. Whenever Holden tells us why he doesn't like someone or something he invariably exaggerates.

Vague expression

The way in which Holden expresses his feelings and emotions is made deliberately vague by the author. Holden often says he doesn't know why he likes things or that he doesn't know why he said a particular thing to someone. He frequently tells us what he is thinking, but does not seem able to draw any conclusions from his thoughts. Whether we agree or not, this tendency to vague expression is often associated with teenagers.

On a number of occasions his descriptions of what is happening to him emotionally are summed up in one word, 'stuff' and he tells us things make him sad or 'blue as hell' but he cannot explain why. His inability to express his emotions clearly is very noticeable at the climax of his story when he is watching Phoebe on the carrousel. Holden tells us he is so happy but can't express these feelings in words. Think of how often you want to explain how you are feeling to someone and the words just don't seem to be there! This is yet another way in which Salinger creates an authentic voice for a teenager.

Use of dialogue

Salinger makes great use of dialogue in the book. One of the main ways that the reader gets an impression of the different characters is by the way they speak and what they say. He doesn't make great use of description in the conventional sense. Descriptions of characters' appearances are kept to a minimum but we get a real feeling for them by their langauge. Think of Maurice the doorman as an example of this technique. We realise he is a rather sordid character by what he says, not by how Salinger describes him. This is also true of Mr Antolini. Rather than telling us he is eloquent and thoughtful, Salinger allows his conversation with Holden to show us.

The other benefit of dialogue – or direct speech – is that it creates a feeling that we are meeting the characters with Holden.

DID YOU KNOW?

When the book was first published in Britain, *The Catholic Herald* condemned its 'formidably excessive use of amateur swearing and coarse language'.

Literary language

The narrative style consciously avoids many of the devices we associate with 'literature': there is little use of **metaphor** and not much 'elegant writing' or detailed description of places or emotions and feelings.

Normally writers create these effects by using adjectives and adverbs or descriptive words. By keeping the use of long descriptive phrases to a minimum, J.D. Salinger persuades us we really are seeing the world through the eyes of a sixteen-year-old.

Sentence structure

Another stylistic feature of the book is the structure of the sentences. Unlike many more literary styles that you may have come across in your reading, Salinger uses mainly simple sentences that are often short. Sometimes the sentences are constructed quite loosely. Often they don't seem to be properly constructed, grammatical sentences, for example, 'It really was.' Salinger sometimes uses punctuation to give the rhythm of speech to his writing. This again creates the effect of a spoken style rather than a literary, written style.

**CHECK
THE BOOK**
J.D. Salinger's
*Seymour: An
Introduction* will
help you to
understand his view
of the world, and
Seymour echoes
aspects of Holden
Caulfield.

AUTHORIAL INTENTION

The way in which J.D. Salinger reveals the world through Holden's individual voice is very clever. By giving Holden a limited ability to describe his world in a sophisticated way, he has made Holden seem even more like a real person. All the above techniques and stategies are what Salinger uses to give this impression.

Holden is fixed in our minds as a mixed-up teenager who lacks the sophistication of an adult to describe what is happening to him. If we feel sympathy for Holden – and it would be cruel not to – it is the way in which he has told his story which makes us do so. It is his individual voice created by Salinger that makes him sound so believable.

Now take a break!

PART FOUR

RESOURCES

HOW TO USE QUOTATIONS

Although J.D. Salinger does not allow commercial enterprises to quote from his work, it is very important that *you*, as a student, learn to use quotations properly in your essays in examinations.

One of the secrets of success in writing essays is the way you use quotations. There are five basic principles:

❶ Put inverted commas at the beginning and end of the quotation.

❷ Write the quotation exactly as it appears in the original.

❸ Do not use a quotation that repeats what you have just written.

❹ Use the quotation so that it fits into your sentence.

❺ Keep the quotation as short as possible.

Quotations should be used to develop the line of thought in your essays. Your comment should not duplicate what is in your quotation. Take this quotation from *Macbeth* for example:

Lady Macbeth tells us that she wants her husband to arrive speedily so that she can pour her spirits in his ear, 'Hie thee hither/ That I may pour my spirits in thine ear' (Act I, Scene 5).

Far more effective is to write:

Lady Macbeth tells her husband to arrive speedily so that 'I may pour my spirits in thine ear' (Act I, Scene 5).

However, the most sophisticated way of using the writer's words is to embed them into your sentence.

EXAMINER'S SECRET
In a typical exam you might use as many as eight quotations.

Lady Macbeth tells her husband to hurry to her so that she can 'pour' her 'spirits' into his ear.

When you use quotations in this way, you are demonstrating the ability to use text as evidence to support your ideas – not simply including words from the original to prove you have read it.

COURSEWORK ESSAY

Set aside an hour or so at the start of your work to plan.

 CHECK THE NET
There are a number of websites devoted to *The Catcher in the Rye* which may help you with our studies.

● List all the points you feel are needed to cover the task. Collect page references of information and quotations that will support what you have to say. A helpful tool is the highlighter pen: this saves painstaking copying and enables you to target precisely what you want to use.

● Focus on what you consider to be the main points of the essay. Try to sum up your argument in a single sentence, which could be the closing sentence of your essay. Depending on the essay title, it could be a statement about a character: Phoebe is the character who saves Holden from himself, because she shows him the importance and beauty of childhood and because she is determined to stay with him when he threatens to run away; an opinion about a setting: New York is used to show what is corrupt and wrong with the values of the society which Holden inhabits; or a judgement on a theme: One of the central themes in *The Catcher in the Rye* is the importance of relationships, as Holden spends nearly all his time trying to find meaningful relationships to take the place of the ones he has lost.

● Make a short essay plan. Use the first paragraph to introduce the argument you wish to make. In the following paragraphs develop this argument with details, examples and other possible points of view. Sum up your argument in the last paragraph. Check you have answered the question.

● Write the essay, remembering all the time the central point you are making.

- On completion, go back over what you have written to eliminate careless errors and improve expression. Read it aloud to yourself or to a relative or friend.

If you can, try to type your essay using a word processor. This will allow you to correct and improve your writing without spoiling its appearance.

SITTING THE EXAMINATION

Examination papers are carefully designed to give you the opportunity to do your best. Follow these handy hints for exam success:

BEFORE YOU START

- Make sure you know the subject of the examination so that you are properly prepared and equipped.

- You need to be comfortable and free from distractions. Inform the invigilator if anything is off-putting, e.g. a shaky desk.

- Read the instructions, or rubric, on the front of the examination paper. You should know by now what you have to do but check to reassure yourself.

- Observe the time allocation – and follow it carefully. If they recommend 60 minutes for Question 1 and 30 minutes for Question 2, it is because Question 1 carries twice as many marks.

- Consider the mark allocation. You should write a longer response for 4 marks than for 2 marks.

WRITING YOUR RESPONSES

- Use the questions to structure your response, e.g. question: 'The endings of X's poems are always particularly significant. Explain their importance with reference to two poems.' The first part of your answer will describe the ending of the first poem; the second part will look at the ending of the second poem; the third part will be an explanation of the significance of the two endings.

EXAMINER'S SECRET
Don't waste time looking around to see how your friends are doing.

CHECK THE NET

The BBC 'Bitesize' pages give helpful revision advice.

- Write a brief draft outline of your response.

- A typical 30-minute examination essay is probably between 400 and 600 words in length.

- Keep your writing legible and easy to read, using paragraphs to show the structure of your answers.

- Spend a couple of minutes afterwards quickly checking for obvious errors.

WHEN YOU HAVE FINISHED

- Don't be downhearted – if you found the examination difficult, it is probably because you really worked at the questions. Let's face it, they are not meant to be easy!

- Don't pay too much attention to what your friends have to say about the paper. Everyone's experience is different and no two people ever give the same answers.

IMPROVE YOUR GRADE

Before discussing particular ways of improving your grade, also read the sections preceding this one on **Coursework essay** and **Sitting the examination**. Many of the points contained there will help you to improve your grade. Here we can go over some of the key general points. These relate to both coursework grades and exam grades.

EXAMINER'S SECRET

Candidates who score highest demonstrate a thorough knowledge of the text.

- Read through the text thoroughly. You should have read the text at least twice before attempting the exam or the coursework piece.

- Use your York Notes wisely! Look at the Check the Book/Film marginal notes and do some research, gathering notes and information to help with your revision.

- Make sure you plan your response to the question carefully. In an exam this can be a list of points relating to the different aspects of the question. For a coursework essay the plan can be more detailed.

- When writing a coursework essay remember to redraft your initial answer. Use your teachers' knowledge and get them to help you to revise and restructure the work.

- Always answer the question! Don't be tempted to say all you know about the book. Candidates who get A and B grades are always focused on the question being asked.

- Don't be tempted to memorise or copy information directly from another source. There are many 'essays' on the internet but the examiner can spot when a student's work isn't in their own words. Don't copy!

- Your grade will improve if you can explain how Salinger uses language. Pay attention to the **Language and style** section of these Notes to help you understand how to do this.

- Make sure you have paid close attention to spelling, punctuation and grammar. While this may not be the main focus of assessment, it will make a good impression on the examiner.

- Include brief quotations from the text to support your answer. The quotations must be relevant to the point you are making. Don't make your quotations overlong. A- or B-grade candidates will integrate their quotations into the point they are making.

Let's look at a specific question to see the difference between particular grades. This question is taken from the sample questions section.

Does J.D. Salinger create a believable character in Holden Caulfield?

The difference between a C-grade and a D-grade candidate's response to this type of question can often be seen at the beginning of their answer. D-grade candidates may start by explaining what happens to Holden in the book. What they are doing is simply retelling the story. To get to the C grade you need to say something about how the character is made believable by the writer.

EXAMINER'S SECRET
The most common cause of poor grades is failure to answer the question set.

EXAMINER'S SECRET
A candidate who is capable of arriving at unusual, well-supported judgements, *independently* is likely to receive the highest marks.

D-grade beginning – Holden gets expelled and goes to New York. This is believable because it's a real place and people get expelled from school in real life. When Holden is in New York he doesn't like it, some people don't like certain places.

C-grade beginning – Holden is a believable character because Salinger makes him sound like a real person talking to us. He uses slang and has his own expressions like 'it killed me'. Salinger shows things happening to Holden that could happen to a teenager of that time.

Notice how the C-grade candidate mentions that the writer is creating the character. This is what the question asks. The C-grade candidate tells us something about Salinger's style although not in the depth required to get to a higher grade.

EXAMINER'S SECRET

You will improve your grade by showing that you are aware that the writer is creating the book. You are discussing his or her work in your response.

In order to progress up the grades you need to have more depth to your introductory remarks. A-grade candidates would show the examiner that they are aware of some of the techniques (see **Language and style**) that Salinger uses to create the character. Their response may begin something like this:

A-grade beginning – Salinger makes Holden believable by giving him an individual voice. Holden uses informal language and speaks directly to the reader at the beginning of the novel by addressing them as 'you'. This makes it seem as if the character is speaking to the reader personally.

The next stage of the answer to this question would require you to develop points that show how Holden is developed as a **persona**.

D-grade candidates may carry on explaining what happens to Holden throughout the story and that the things he goes through are believable. They may mention that Salinger brings in Holden's memories of times gone by, that he talks about his family and so on. While this will get the candidate marks it will not be sufficient to get to a C grade.

A C-grade candidate would make some more specific points about Holden's surroundings and may mention some of characters Holden meets as an example of how Holden's experiences are like those of a real person. For example:

C grade – Holden's experiences seem believable to the reader. For example Holden meets many people who don't understand him, like the taxi drivers in New York, Sally Hayes and Mr Antolini. This helps us see that Holden is mixed up and confused.

An A-grade candidate might discuss the way Salinger links different parts of the text to create Holden's character. and show how Holden's responses are consistent:

A grade – Many of the characters whom Holden meets do not understand him, for example Mr Spencer, Sally Hayes and Mr Antolini. Holden is shown to be isolated from their views and unable to communicate effectively with them. This echoes the beginning of the book where Holden describes being alone on the hill at school. The whole novel shows a character who is misunderstood and alone, this is how Salinger creates sympathy for Holden, who could be viewed as an unpleasant character.

Notice how the candidate links this response back to the question while clearly explaining his/her views on Holden's character. The A-grade candidate is showing his/her understanding of Salinger's purpose and an awareness of the importance of the structure of the book.

EXAMINER'S SECRET
A high-grade candidate will show how different parts of the book link together.

In order to develop the answer further you would need to consider Holden's voice in more detail as this is the main way Salinger creates a believable character. A C- or D- grade candidate may mention that Holden uses slang that was around at the time of writing. They may mention Holden's tendency to exaggerate and swear. The C-grade answer would probably support these points with some examples of Holden's language from the text.

D grade – Holden uses swear words and slang all through the book. He can't explain himself very well like a lot of teenagers.

C grade – Holden uses slang and swear words throughout the book, for example, 'witty bastards', 'tossed his cookies'. Holden can't explain his emotions very well as, for example, when he talks about sex in Chapter 9. This makes him sound like a real teenager.

EXAMINER'S SECRET

Always support your points with examples from the text and then explain their significance.

A-grade candidates would focus more on how the writer creates his voice. They would develop their point from their opening comments.

A grade – Salinger maintains the individuality of Holden's character by using the slang of the time, 'tossed his cookies', 'blue as hell' and also by taboo language to shock the reader, for example, 'witty bastard' and 'my ass'. Holden cannot express his feelings very well, like many teenagers, particularly when discussing feelings. This is a clever technique as it reinforces Holden's immaturity and makes him appear to be a 'normal' teenager.

To sum up, high-grade candidates will demonstrate a clear understanding of the requirements of the question and use quotations and examples to back up their points. A- and B-grade candidates will be able to structure and develop their own ideas and also give their own opinion about the text.

C-grade candidates also do these things but may not have the same degree of depth to their answer. They may rely more on telling the reader what happens but they will back up their points with evidence from the text. You must show examples from the book and answer the question if you are to have a chance of progressing from the D grade to the C grade.

SAMPLE ESSAY PLAN

A typical essay question on *The Catcher in the Rye* is followed by a sample essay plan in note form. This does not present the only answer to the question, merely one answer. Do not be afraid to include you own ideas, and leave out some of those in the sample!

Remember, it is essential to use material from the novel to prove and illustrate the points you make.

What do you think are the reasons for Holden's breakdown?

Introduction

Holden tells us about his current circumstances and we realise he has a problem. Outline Holden's worsening condition as his story develops.

Part 1: Pencey Prep

- Holden is presented as someone who does not fit in. He has been expelled from school – the beginning of his problems.

- Describe his inability to apply himself to schoolwork and his lack of real friends in the school.

- Mention his brother Allie's death and the effects this may have had on Holden.

- Mention the fight with Stradlater and how it indicates his anger at the world in which he lives.

Part 2: Attitudes to people

- Outline Holden's attitude towards the people he meets, particularly his tendency to think of people as phony.

- Discuss Holden's loneliness and how he becomes depressed by people's behaviour.

- Comment on how Holden is alienated from people around him and the effect this may have on his mental state.

Part 3: Attitudes towards society

- Holden cannot understand the way society seems to work and feels that there is much unfairness in the world.

- Mention his feelings about religion and the fact that society seems hypocritical.

- Discuss how this may contribute to Holden's mental state.

 **EXAMINER'S SECRET**
If you are going to use literary terms like **irony** and **anti-hero**, make sure you know what they mean and can offer examples from the book.

Part 4: Guilt

- Holden feels guilt about many things he does.

- Discuss his feelings about his parents and their reaction to his expulsion from yet another school.

- Mention his attempts to behave like an adult and his inability to do so.

EXAMINER'S SECRET

When studying and revising, identify some key quotations which may be used for a variety of possible essays.

- Comment on his relationship with his sister and her fears about him.

Part 5: Conclusion

- Life seems pointless to him after the death of his brother.

- He could not reconcile this with the demands people placed on him. Everything else seemed unimportant or shallow to him.

- What caused his breakdown was people's expectations of him.

- His worsening mental state is mirrored in the novel by his worsening material state, i.e. running out of money, sleeping rough, getting drunk.

- The emotional turmoil Holden experiences is responsible for his breakdown. This is the main reason for his stay in the hospital in California.

- The lasting impression is that Holden went through a period of his life where he could not cope with the pressures of growing up.

FURTHER QUESTIONS

Make a plan as shown above and attempt these questions.

1. What does the novel tell us about school?
2. How does Holden's way of telling his story affect our response?
3. Holden tries hard to act 'grown up' in the novel. Does he succeed?

4 Why is Jane Gallagher an important character in the novel?

5 Do you think Phoebe helps Holden to face his parents?

6 Why can't Holden 'fit in', either at school or in New York?

7 Does J.D. Salinger create a believable character in Holden Caulfield?

8 What is the importance of the title of the book?

9 'All Holden's experiences with the opposite sex are negative.' Do you agree?

10 Do you sympathise with Holden Caulfield?

Now take a break!

anti-hero an unheroic protagonist of a play or novel; a character whose attractiveness or interest consists of their inability to perform deeds of bravery or courage. Do not let the term 'anti' suggest to you that they are necessarily bad

bildungsroman a novel which describes the main character's development from childhood to maturity, focusing on the relationship between experience, education, character and identity

closure the impression of completeness and finality achieved by the ending of some literary works, for example 'they lived happily ever after' and 'Reader, I married him'. *The Catcher in the Rye*, like many other twentieth-century novels, has an 'open' ending which refuses to leave the reader comfortably satisfied and leaves the text open to multiple interpretations

episodic a type of narrative which is written in the simple form of a series of more or less separable or discrete episodes or incidents, rather than a complicated and involved plot

first-person narrative a story told in the first-person singular (an 'I' figure who is directly involved)

flashback a sudden jump backwards in time to an earlier episode, giving the reader a fuller picture as the past is described as well as the present. This term is borrowed from films – perhaps demonstrating Holden's familiarity with the cinema?

frame narrative the outer, containing story, which is a pretext for the more significant narrative embedded within it

image something described by the writer to create a particular mental impression in the reader

ironic saying one thing while meaning another

metaphor one thing described as another thing, thus 'carrying over' its associations

persona the voice in a story written in the first person.

point of view the way in which the narrator approaches his or her material (characters, action, setting etc.) and audience

protagonist the leading character (or characters) in a novel or play

realism in literature, writing in such a way that represents things as common sense perceives them to be. Realism focuses on individuals rather than stereotypes

symbol something which represents something else by analogy or association. Holden's red hunting hat has symbolic value in *The Catcher in the Rye* (see **Structure**)

CHECKPOINT 1 It helps to create a sense of mystery about the narrator and encourages us to read on.

CHECKPOINT 2 Holden cannot see the value of education. It is an early example of him as a rebel.

CHECKPOINT 3 Holden doesn't conform to other people's sets of values. He should see himself as privileged and this is what baffles people.

CHECKPOINT 4 They both have an unhappy childhood but in different ways.

CHECKPOINT 5 With Maurice the elevator man.

CHECKPOINT 6 Yes, in one way, but he also wants to protect Jane from Stradlater who he feels will corrupt her.

CHECKPOINT 7 It is a technique used by Salinger to create the impression of Holden as an immature teenage boy.

CHECKPOINT 8 His lying makes us think he would like to be someone else.

CHECKPOINT 9 He seems to want a link back to happier times but may be afraid that Jane has changed and his 'perfect memory' will be shattered.

CHECKPOINT 10 Apart from the fact they are brothers and sister, they all tell (or write) stories.

CHECKPOINT 11 She is the closest he has to a true friend. All through the novel we see Holden trying to connect with people and failing.

CHECKPOINT 12 People are pretending to enjoy themselves, they are not being genuine.

CHECKPOINT 13 The nuns represent the opposite values to most of the people Holden knows. Unlike the people in the nightclub, they seem genuine.

CHECKPOINT 14 Like many other characters, she cannot undersand why Holden goes against the world she lives in. She is happy with her life.

CHECKPOINT 15 He escapes from school early in Chapter 8. He says he wants to join a monastery in Chapter 7.

CHECKPOINT 16 Yes. Once again, Holden cannot communicate clearly.

CHECKPOINT 17 Once again Sally is being used as a substitute for Jane Gallagher. Holden is lonely and drunk. This does show his shallow side.

CHECKPOINT 18 Allie in Chapter 5 and also James Castle in Chapter 22.

CHECKPOINT 19 Perhaps because he doesn't want her to make the same mistakes as he does. He is proud of Phoebe.

CHECKPOINT 20 Holden says he doesn't mind being caught but then hides from his mother.

CHECKPOINT 21 He mentions he is breathless in Chapter 21 and also says he feels ill at Mr Antolini's house.

TEST YOURSELF (CHAPTERS 1–7)

1 Mr Spencer

2 Mal Brossard and Robert Ackley

3 Three

4 Edgar Marsalla farting

5 His brother Allie's baseball mitt

6 Because of his bad health and personal habits

7 Because Stradlater complains about the essay Holden has written, then attacks his personality, and finally aggravates Holden by not revealing details of his date with Jane Gallagher

TEST YOURSELF (CHAPTERS 8–14)

1 Mrs Morrow

2 Bernice, Marty and Laverne

3 Ernie

4 Sunny

5 The Lavender Room and Ernie's

6 Maine

7 An argument over money

TEST YOURSELF (CHAPTERS 15–20)

1 Sally Hayes

2 Miss Aigletinger

3 The Lunts

4 Carl Luce

5 *Romeo and Juliet*

6 *Little Shirley Beans*

7 The Wicker Bar

TEST YOURSELF (CHAPTERS 21–26)

1 James Castle

2 Benedict Arnold

3 A party in Norwalk, Connecticut

4 Robert Burns

5 Highballs

6 Grand Central Station

7 The zoo and the park

Maya Angelou
I Know Why the Caged Bird Sings

Jane Austen
Pride and Prejudice

Alan Ayckbourn
Absent Friends

Elizabeth Barrett Browning
Selected Poems

Robert Bolt
A Man for All Seasons

Harold Brighouse
Hobson's Choice

Charlotte Brontë
Jane Eyre

Emily Brontë
Wuthering Heights

Shelagh Delaney
A Taste of Honey

Charles Dickens
David Copperfield
Great Expectations
Hard Times
Oliver Twist

Roddy Doyle
Paddy Clarke Ha Ha Ha

George Eliot
Silas Marner
The Mill on the Floss

Anne Frank
The Diary of a Young Girl

William Golding
Lord of the Flies

Oliver Goldsmith
She Stoops to Conquer

Willis Hall
The Long and the Short and the Tall

Thomas Hardy
Far from the Madding Crowd

The Mayor of Casterbridge
Tess of the d'Urbervilles
The Withered Arm and other Wessex Tales

L.P. Hartley
The Go-Between

Seamus Heaney
Selected Poems

Susan Hill
I'm the King of the Castle

Barry Hines
A Kestrel for a Knave

Louise Lawrence
Children of the Dust

Harper Lee
To Kill a Mockingbird

Laurie Lee
Cider with Rosie

Arthur Miller
The Crucible
A View from the Bridge

Robert O'Brien
Z for Zachariah

Frank O'Connor
My Oedipus Complex and Other Stories

George Orwell
Animal Farm

J.B. Priestley
An Inspector Calls
When We Are Married

Willy Russell
Educating Rita
Our Day Out

J.D. Salinger
The Catcher in the Rye

William Shakespeare
Henry IV Part I
Henry V
Julius Caesar

Macbeth
The Merchant of Venice
A Midsummer Night's Dream
Much Ado About Nothing
Romeo and Juliet
The Tempest
Twelfth Night

George Bernard Shaw
Pygmalion

Mary Shelley
Frankenstein

R.C. Sherriff
Journey's End

Rukshana Smith
Salt on the snow

John Steinbeck
Of Mice and Men

Robert Louis Stevenson
Dr Jekyll and Mr Hyde

Jonathan Swift
Gulliver's Travels

Robert Swindells
Daz 4 Zoe

Mildred D. Taylor
Roll of Thunder, Hear My Cry

Mark Twain
Huckleberry Finn

James Watson
Talking in Whispers

Edith Wharton
Ethan Frome

William Wordsworth
Selected Poems

A Choice of Poets

Mystery Stories of the Nineteenth Century including The Signalman

Nineteenth Century Short Stories

Poetry of the First World War

Six Women Poets

Margaret Atwood
Cat's Eye
The Handmaid's Tale

Jane Austen
Emma
Mansfield Park
Persuasion
Pride and Prejudice
Sense and Sensibility

Alan Bennett
Talking Heads

William Blake
Songs of Innocence and of Experience

Charlotte Brontë
Jane Eyre
Villette

Emily Brontë
Wuthering Heights

Angela Carter
Nights at the Circus

Geoffrey Chaucer
The Franklin's Prologue and Tale
The Miller's Prologue and Tale
The Prologue to the Canterbury Tales
The Wife of Bath's Prologue and Tale

Samuel Coleridge
Selected Poems

Joseph Conrad
Heart of Darkness

Daniel Defoe
Moll Flanders

Charles Dickens
Bleak House
Great Expectations
Hard Times

Emily Dickinson
Selected Poems

John Donne
Selected Poems

Carol Ann Duffy
Selected Poems

George Eliot
Middlemarch
The Mill on the Floss

T.S. Eliot
Selected Poems
The Waste Land

F. Scott Fitzgerald
The Great Gatsby

E.M. Forster
A Passage to India

Brian Friel
Translations

Thomas Hardy
Jude the Obscure
The Mayor of Casterbridge
The Return of the Native
Selected Poems
Tess of the d'Urbervilles

Seamus Heaney
Selected Poems from 'Opened Ground'

Nathaniel Hawthorne
The Scarlet Letter

Homer
The Iliad
The Odyssey

Aldous Huxley
Brave New World

Kazuo Ishiguro
The Remains of the Day

Ben Jonson
The Alchemist

James Joyce
Dubliners

John Keats
Selected Poems

Christopher Marlowe
Doctor Faustus
Edward II

Arthur Miller
Death of a Salesman

John Milton
Paradise Lost Books I & II

Toni Morrison
Beloved

George Orwell
Nineteen Eighty-Four

Sylvia Plath
Selected Poems

Alexander Pope
Rape of the Lock & Selected Poems

William Shakespeare
Antony and Cleopatra
As You Like It
Hamlet
Henry IV Part I
King Lear
Macbeth
Measure for Measure
The Merchant of Venice
A Midsummer Night's Dream
Much Ado About Nothing
Othello
Richard II
Richard III
Romeo and Juliet
The Taming of the Shrew
The Tempest
Twelfth Night
The Winter's Tale

George Bernard Shaw
Saint Joan

Mary Shelley
Frankenstein

Jonathan Swift
Gulliver's Travels and A Modest Proposal

Alfred Tennyson
Selected Poems

Virgil
The Aeneid

Alice Walker
The Color Purple

Oscar Wilde
The Importance of Being Earnest

Tennessee Williams
A Streetcar Named Desire

Jeanette Winterson
Oranges Are Not the Only Fruit

John Webster
The Duchess of Malfi

Virginia Woolf
To the Lighthouse

W.B. Yeats
Selected Poems

Metaphysical Poets